CHOR
CANADA:

WILLIAM D. GAIRDNER

OH, OH, CANADA!

A VOICE FROM THE CONSERVATIVE RESISTANCE

Published by
BPS Books
Toronto, Canada
www.bpsbooks.net
A division of Bastian Publishing Services Ltd.

ISBN 978-0-9784402-9-9

Cataloguing in Publication Data available from Library and Archives Canada

Cover design: Greg Devitt Design
Text design and typesetting: Greg Devitt Design

Dedicated with love and affection to the wonderful grandchildren I have already — Jackson, Ethan, Walker, Austin, and Mason — and to all those yet to come

CONTENTS

PREFACE

When I was a young boy, a wise old man told me there were two ways to answer a serious question. "You can give a first-order answer," he said, "which is what most people do, in the hope that they will not have to work any harder. Or, you can decide to do the work, and find a second-order answer."

"What is the difference?" I asked, and he answered by pointing to a radio sitting on the desk beside him, one of those older types with a cover, a dial, and a few rotating buttons.

"If I asked you how this radio works," he said, "you could give what most people would say is a perfectly good and perfectly true answer by showing how to turn it on, like this." He reached for the first dial and turned it on. Then he twiddled another dial and found a pleasant music station. Smiling, he said, "You see? That's how the radio works. On-off, volume control, station-finder, and so on. Most people who see me do this will never ask how a radio works again, and will never want to know anything more about it. My answer is good and true, but for the really curious person is not very satisfying. It tells how the radio *operates* but does not say how it really *works*."

At this point he lifted the cover off the radio and showed me something I had never seen before: a little jungle of glowing vacuum tubes and a tangle of coloured wires and all sorts of other gizmos soldered together that had always been hidden from view just because I had never bothered to take a radio apart myself. Then he gave me what he called a second-order answer to the question. I must admit, I was enthralled, because what he told me seemed like magic. He explained about radio waves, and how they were invented, and when, and by whom, and how they travel through the air at various frequencies and even pass through our bodies, and how they hit the radio antenna — here it is, right here, he showed me — and how this and that tube (which had to be a vacuum, I can't remember why) would convert the radio wave into the sounds of the beautiful music I was hearing at that very moment.

I remember asking him, "But how, but how *really*?" And I knew at that very moment that he had hooked me. I have never thought about a radio — or much else — in quite the same way since.

Now this little story is just my way of saying that although he is long gone now, this lovely old man is still with me, like a voice encouraging me to take the cover off whatever subject I am writing about in order to give readers a satisfying, second-order experience.

That is all I have tried to do in every essay in this book. It is my fond hope that after reading them my readers will join the resistance by never accepting less.

I

Culture

LATE NIGHT THOUGHTS ON EQUALITY

Today, no word is more used and less understood than "equality."

Why do our minds automatically reach for it as if for a gun to force a point or defend ourselves against some injustice? And when we use it in this way, what do we mean? What did we *ever* mean? And on what personal experience of equality are we drawing? For a moment's reflection reveals that nothing is "equal" to anything else. Not any two apples, two cars, or two people. Neither can we appeal to history, for our contemporary conception of equality — at least so it seems to me — is unique. In what follows, I will try to follow the threads of this concept as it kept me awake last night.

The ancient Greeks and Romans had their own versions of equality and would have ridiculed ours. The Greeks drew lots for many political offices. At certain points in their history, they viewed all citizens as supposedly equally available for office by lot (except for certain war offices). But the true Greek idea of equality was *equality by rank*: All soldiers must be treated the same as one another. All generals the same as one another. All Senators the same, all slaves the same, and so on. The Greeks never for a moment believed that these ranks and classes of people and ability were "equal" to each other, except before the law: a noble and a commoner ought to be given the same punishment for stealing, for example.

But even in the most radical form of Greek democracy under Demosthenes, the Athenian Senate — called the *Boule*

3

— made the laws and passed them *down* to the people for their acceptance or rejection. The legislative "initiative" was with the older and the wiser, not with the common people, for they were not considered "equal" to their wiser elders (the minimum age for Boule membership was thirty). The Greeks would have ridiculed the idea of making legislation and passing it *up* to older and wiser Senators, as we do. And needless to say, slaves were not equal to citizens. It was the same in Rome, where all citizens had the same rights, but social classes were quite distinct, and slaves (at one point in the Empire's slow decline, an estimated seventy-five percent of all Romans had some slave ancestry!) had applied to them a special form of category law not used for full citizens.

Our modern sense of democracy — and equality — was a child of the Reformation of the sixteenth century. It was a Christian artifact born of the idea that humans in the Garden of Eden before the Fall were pure, sinless, all the same, and equal, holding all the goods of the Earth in common and equally. It was, if you like, a Judeo-Christian vision of a communism that we once lived and would live again. Radical Christian reformers used to protest that we should return to that condition, so that here on Earth there should be no *meum* and *teum* (mine and thine). Some of them took this protest in the name of common property so far that they started preying sexually on other men's wives, on the supposed religious grounds that no one has a right to a woman for their sole private pleasure!

At any rate, some three centuries later, after the rise of industrial prosperity, when Western society as a whole began to lurch toward increasing materialism and atheism, the connection with that religiously engendered ideal of human equality — with the possibility of a selfless spiritual grace unencumbered by differences — simply got replaced by what was left over: claims for an equal distribution of material things and equal personal rights, minus the spiritual grace, thank you very much.

For centuries there was a slow transition from the civic form of democracy that we had under the influence of a more reasonable Christianity, which lasted until the very early part of the twentieth century, to our present form of secular democracy, which I call "hyperdemocracy." The earlier form accepted that all humans are different, and if in some sense they are the same or equal, it is obviously only in the eyes of God and before the law. Social and class differences were a fact of life, and true equality was to be found only in the afterlife. Indeed, in that world, the various rankings of ability, intelligence, wisdom, and wealth were expected to determine the roles of artisan, farmer, soldier, statesman, noble, teacher, priest, and so on. And it was widely feared that an insistence on radical equality would devastate the harmonious interaction of these degrees of rank, ability, and character, and bring civilization down. Democracy in that epoch, resting on a myriad of such fruitfully interacting inequalities, was assumed to reflect the moral consensus of the whole people. From the late eighteenth century forward, the French Revolution was sufficient evidence for most that at the end of the road to forced equality loomed the shadow of the guillotine.

Very recently this moral consensus on democracy has been replaced by the hyperdemocratic idea that democratic rights are not inherent in society as a whole, but in ourselves as individuals. So at once morality, too, became thought of as something to be decided by individuals, and no longer as something formed by a moral and social consensus that hovers over us as an edict for personal behaviour. We stopped thinking of "the body politic" or of society as something greater than the sum of its parts. Rather, we began to believe — we all now take it as an article of faith — that the parts are all there is and therefore all that

5

matters. There is no whole any longer. (And if someone says there is, who in modern Canada dares speak for it?)

It was this transition that set us all up as equal individual claimants on welfare states conceived as mere administrative entities expected to deliver the goods equally to all. No one expects equality in the afterlife any longer. So let's arrange it now, was the conclusion: by force, taxation, legislation, and court edicts. In other words, let's get equality from the law, the state, and our neighbours. Forevermore the debates would focus not on working together for some common moral vision of the good, but on rankings of individual rights to what we think we — or, when we have the energy to organize others for personal gain, what we think our petty little interest groups — deserve.

All that remained was to write a Charter of Rights and Freedoms (with no mention of duties or responsibilities) as a kind of national promissory note to ourselves to facilitate and guarantee that vision. That is how the notion of equality, driven forward by this secular bible called the Charter, changed our national home into a motel.

STICKS AND STONES

When I was young, boys and girls used to taunt each other mercilessly at recess. Sometimes it was from real anger; sometimes it was just a kind of cover-up for some secret but unrequited affection. And of course no boy who wanted to live until lunchtime would ever hit a girl. Violence against girls was always verbal. And the girls had a kind of primordial response. It was a verse taught to them by their mothers, which they always sang with a taunting cheerfulness, and which, as far as we boys were concerned, was conclusively and irritatingly unanswerable: "Sticks and stones will break my bones, but words will never hurt me."

Today I figure that verse must have been some kind of powerful cultural lesson speaking through the girls, teaching us that words and the actions they ordinarily imply can always be separated or neutralized; *that words have as much truth and power over you, or hurt value, as you are willing to allow them.* The implication was that there is no reason to accept the face-value meaning of words or statements unconditionally or automatically unless you wish to, because if you do, then whoever utters them will be able to control your emotions, and therefore your life, at will. You would become their puppet, a victim of their every word and whim.

The sticks and stones verse was a powerfully protective schoolyard antidote to what might be called the primitive, or "magic," view of language that everyone sensed was an ever-present danger, one that, once embraced (invariably in a moment of anger), would also be a concession to one's own darkest animal nature. For the magic view of language is an almost certain mark of a primitive society and a primitive person, and it is likely to be found at the early stages of all civilizations, as it is in the earliest years of a child's life. It is the belief that with words, chants, hexes, curses, incantations, and other sorts of mumbo-jumbo, we can control others (or they, us), and maybe even future events.

At least as recently as the immediate post–World War II era, that verse was known by virtually all children and amounted to a deeply embedded public philosophy of the liberal-democratic Western world, to the effect that in order for ordinary words to be considered seriously, they must have some proven connection with truth. Until then, they are just sticks and stones that will bounce off you unnoticed as if made of sponge, with the poor thrower left an object of pity.

In this respect, I remember in the late 1960s staring in disbelief at a *Life* magazine double-spread photograph of an immense black horde of tunic-clad Chinese students, perhaps a million of them, all chanting and waving their copies of the Little Red Book of Mao Tse-tung with rabid fervour. I remember my feeling of pity as for an inferior form of life, or a sick dog, for here was a whole people trapped in what we now call "political correctness." It was unimaginable then that we would ever stoop to such base mob-think. It was clear that they had no conception of political or language freedom, and that every "saying" was loaded with a pre-determined significance that could be contradicted only at the risk of personal peril. It was, and is, also clear that such totalitarian societies are marked by their entrapment in or (if they were once free) reversion to a magic view of language.

It seems that we, too — with the loss of religious sentiment and the ideal of transcendent truth that usually accompanies it, along with the rise of secularism, materialism, and, let's face it, our own brand of socialism — have reverted to the magic view of words.

So my worry now is the company we are keeping, because all totalitarian regimes cling to a magic view of language, and we have now begun doing this ourselves. In his sobering book *Death by Government*, Professor R.J. Rummel of the University of Hawaii, one of the few authorities on how many human beings have been killed, slaughtered, gassed, or starved by various totalitarian regimes (Nazi, Soviet, Chinese, Khmer Rouge, etc.), tells us, in chapter 6, "The Nazi Genocide State," that in addition to the "six million" Jews (his quotation marks, not mine, indicating the figure is to his mind historically unverified),

> the Nazis murdered somewhere between 15,000,000 and 31,000,000 people, most likely closer to 21 million men, women, handicapped, aged, sick, prisoners of war, forced laborers, camp inmates, critics, homosexuals, Jews, Slavs, Serbs, Czechs, Italians, Poles, Frenchmen, Ukrainians, and so on. Among them were 1 million children under eighteen years of age.

The Soviet Gulag deserves a special place in history for the greatest number of killings. The total for that regime, Rummel says, is 61,911,000. The total given for the "lesser megamurderers" is 19,178,000, divided between the Chinese, Japanese, Cambodians, Turks, Poles, Yugoslavs, North Koreans, and so on. All had horrific genocidal regimes of one kind or another.

Perhaps the most shocking conclusion of Rummel's work, however, is that *government is bad for your health*: he shows that in all the wars of the twentieth century, some fifty million military combatants died. That is terrible enough. But at least they died fighting enemies of their countries. They were trying to protect their loved ones and their nations. The real shocker is his confirmation that *one hundred and sixty-seven million non-combatants, all full legal citizens, were killed by their own governments.* And that is just the confirmed number. He suspects that the real, but unverifiable, number is almost double.

It is a simple fact of history that all these killer regimes took great pains to codify, and then punish citizens with torture or death, for misusing the state's official political conception of language-as-magic. Perhaps we ought to think about that. Or better yet, if we want to start removing our own totalitarian language mentality, we ought, once again, to teach our kids: "Sticks and stones will break my bones, but words will never hurt me."

DYING FOR VALUES

Canadian values, eh? Former Canadian Foreign Affairs diplomat Martin Collacott thinks Ottawa should "demand a more explicit commitment to Canada and Canadian values ..." from new immigrants (with special attention to the Muslim community). This advice comes in the study *Canada's Inadequate Response to Terrorism*, published by the Fraser Institute.

But I think he means liberal values.

A friend of mine from the former Yugoslavia was once hired by the RCMP for some internal spying. He told me, after his stint, how astonished he was to learn that "Canada is crawling with agents who are spying on us, and also on each other." Our daily world sits on top of a shadow world that pops up once in a while and disappears just as quickly.

I saw this once myself at my former business, the Fitness Institute, in Toronto. A black-windowed car pulled up to our building and three men in dark suits pushed their way past our receptionist, on the run, and disappeared down our hallway into the locker room. Who in the *&$%& was that, I asked myself, as I ran after them somewhat cautiously. Gone. I mean, they disappeared into our building somewhere, somehow, and were never seen again, and when I got back to the front door the car had vanished. Shadows.

As for the "liberal-democratic" values that new immigrants are encouraged to learn? More shadows there. My godfather, Bill Weis, joined the Royal Canadian Air Force during World War II and died for what he was convinced were Canada's liberal-democratic values. He was last seen diving out of control into a dark forest south of Paris with a five-hundred-pound bomb strapped to his aircraft. I still have the mournful letter from Ottawa, informing his family, with regret, that "no remains were to be found." Well, that man was fighting for "Canadian values," and he lost his life for them. It is sobering to ask what those values were.

In brief, they were that Canada would never become a nation that succumbed to any form of statist socialism such as was then menacing Europe (but such as we now endure through various programs of "redistribution" to myriad classes of people, and from giver to taker provinces); to ensure that our traditional bottom-up style, Parliament-made law — which was always considered "the supreme law of the land" — would never surrender to any top-down control of the laws or the people (by unelected judges who think it is their right to read their personal social preferences into the abstract words of a charter); to ensure that Canada would never lose its respect for the division of powers that made our original constitution so unique (and which has since been foiled by the central government bribing all our provinces into socialist schemes with its "shared-cost" programs); to ensure that we would always revere and protect our ancient customs, rights, and traditions — as old as Magna Carta — such as a citizen's right to private property (private property is not protected in our Charter); to ensure that the people's ancient right to free enterprise not be eroded by governments setting up competitive enterprises that drive the people out of business (Canada then had less than one hundred Crown Corporations, and now has over twelve hundred spread federally and provincially); and not least, to ensure that government does not enslave present or future citizens with public debt beyond what can be paid off by each generation (Canada in 1945 had a mere $16 billion of federal debt, accumulated over the seventy-eight years since Confederation).

On that last point, consider that, today, Canada carries over $550 billion in federal debt alone, which is considered "structural" because it cannot be paid off without ruining the country. Canada also carries billions of dollars in debt in the form of "unfunded liabilities," such as the Canada Pension Plan, which is a debt instead of a resource because no actual pension fund exists. It is a Ponzi, or a Pay-Go, scheme, in which younger workers pay for the retiring old. As a consequence of all this, almost a third of every tax dollar raised in Canada is used to pay debt. In effect, we are asking future generations to pay for our current consumption, just as we are paying for the consumption of our predecessors. This is an immoral obligation laid on all future Canadian children, and one from which they cannot escape. They are born into a fiscal jail.

Like everyone else at the time, Bill Weis thought, as a matter of course, that new immigrants to Canada should be prepared to look after themselves and their families with their own resources; that they should speak passable English on entering, or learn it very fast; and that the central role of God should be recognized in all public places. Like the rest of us, all immigrant schoolchildren were expected to say, every day, before classes began, the Lord's Prayer and sing "God Save the King" (as it was then, with George VI on the throne).

If you ask me, I would say that my godfather would not have recognized the "values" we think are Canadian today, and that if he had learned of them, he might even have figured he was about to die in vain.

CHOMSKY AND NATIVISM

Noam Chomsky is in the news again. This time it is for the reason that despite being the most cited thinker in history after Socrates and Christ, he appears to be a normal human being, capable of blatant hypocrisy. Despite having been a lifelong and stridently bitter critic of capitalism and corporate America (actually, of corporate anything, anywhere, anytime), he has apparently invested his own capitalist millions in solid corporate stocks. I think it is smart to invest money in good companies. But it must be embarrassing for Chomsky to be caught saying one thing and doing another. To walk his own talk, he should either have given his millions away to the poor of the world — which is what he wants all of us to do — or, at the least, to have invested in CastroLite beer stocks, or the MaoMuffin company, thereby supporting his own vaunted socialist ideals.

I don't want to talk about his politics, however, because from what little I know of them, I agree with Martin Peretz's judgment. When editor of *The New Republic*, he simply shook his head at Chomsky's radical ravings and rather charitably concluded that, in this domain at least, Chomsky was "a fool."

My own life has been affected by Chomsky in domains where he may also turn out to be wrong, but in which he is no fool. When I was at Stanford in the 1960s, slogging through a master's degree in structural linguistics, Chomsky's first influential publication, *Syntactic Structures* (1957), landed on my desk. It was a bit of a shock, for like so many others at the time, I had been exposed to lots of behaviourism, determinism, and "blank-slate" theories of the mind that together served as a foundation for the reigning orthodoxies of science and philosophy in the Western world. All were attempts to explain how human beings learn, and all rested on the assumption that the human mind, while it may have a few built-in modalities that make learning itself possible, is basically, from birth, a blank slate waiting for "stimuli" to hit it from the external world of experience. The basic idea was that the human mind is plastic and malleable. Lefties and other tyrants loved — and still love — this idea, because if you believe the mind is plastic, then you can shape it (both the world, and the mind) as you wish. That's why Chomsky, himself a political leftie, called this theory of the mind "a dictator's dream."

This theme haunts us still, courtesy of the superannuated influence of John Locke and the "empirical" tradition. At the time, it had crept into language-learning theory. Children were said to learn language from "motherese" — that is, from the millions of utterances that bombard them from their environment. The reigning theorist of language-learning at the time was B.F. Skinner. In 1957 Skinner published *Verbal Behavior*, which he intended as a flagship statement of the idea that the mind is empty until experience writes on it. Well, in what is still regarded as possibly the most devastating book review in history, Chomsky tore Skinner's book to pieces (in the journal *Language*, vol. 35, 1959). Except for a few hangers-on, some of whom are still hanging on, that review sounded the death knell of behaviourism.

This is where it gets rather interesting, because the blank slate idea always appeals to the left, and the opposing, or "nativist" idea that we are "born that way" always appeals to conservatives.

Chomsky had burst onto the scene with what was actually an older sort of theory, similar to that of René Descartes, who believed that the mind is already equipped by God for learning. Indeed, Chomsky later wrote a fascinating book called *Cartesian Linguistics*. At any rate, Chomsky's new God was the human LAD, or Language Acquisition Device. He referred to this as a "mental organ," and used mathematical and "deep structure" analysis to show that the generation of human linguistic utterances is so amazingly complex that nothing except some kind of LAD could explain how it is possible for a young child (or an adult) to produce an infinite number of novel and grammatically acceptable utterances from a finite number of elements (the limited number of sounds and words in each human language). As compared with the old static sort of grammars from which we learned how to analyze, or "parse," sentences, here was an exciting concept of "transformational" and "generative" grammar that worked out the number of ways in which humans can generate, from finite material, infinite novel utterances that they have never heard before.

It was all very exciting, and still is. My study is cluttered with Chomsky books at the moment because I recently finished writing a chapter on this topic in a new book called *The Book of Absolutes* (to appear in the fall of 2008). The chapter is entitled "The Universals of Language," and the last part of it deals with Chomsky's nativist contribution to this topic. Nativists believe that we do not "learn" language. We "grow" it when we are ready — just as we grow teeth when we are ready — and the biological equipment that enables this development is common to all human beings. It is a universal, and genetically endowed, aspect or capacity of the human brain. (Animals do not come off quite as well, because their languages are so limited, and are not "recursive" systems that generate infinite utterances from finite materials.)

So, in his politics Chomsky is a radical leftist. But in his philosophy of mind he is a conservative, or rightist. Put that together!

For those who want a more or less gentle introduction to this, the best I have found is a book by Neil Smith, *Chomsky: Ideas and Ideals* (Cambridge University Press, 1999). Not surprisingly, Chomsky has many frankly leftist enemies in this field, too, who argue that his theories amount to a kind of linguistic Platonism that is just plain fanciful. They insist that children learn language just like they learn dancing, or how to throw a ball — by repetition of the act. The best book taking this angle is Geoffrey Sampson's *The Language Instinct Debate* (London: Continuum, 1997 and 2005). On this front, at least, the war between Locke and Descartes rages on.

Anthropology and Ethics

In Nova Scotia somewhere is a very interesting Canadian professor, recently retired from Saint Mary's University, named Richard Beis. This professor spends as much time as he can on the golf course, when he is not working at the local food bank. I managed to make contact with him after locating a most interesting article he wrote in 1964, "Some Contributions of Anthropology to Ethics" (*The Thomist*, vol. xxvi, no. 2, April 1964). The article did not receive the attention it deserved in the social-sciences community because it was published in a journal devoted to studies of St. Thomas Aquinas during the secular high tide of cultural and ethical relativism. I am guessing that it would have been turned away by most secular journals.

In any case, I urge readers interested in the topics of ethics, human universals, and natural law to find the article. Beis is a philosopher with a sharp mind who pretty much destroys the underpinnings of philosophical and cultural relativism. But, as I said, this went almost unremarked on in 1964, when hippie-doom was a-blooming.

What Beis revealed is that while the American anthropological establishment largely created the arguments and dug up the (it seems now, very biased and selective) evidence for cultural and ethical relativism, other anthropologists during the same period were providing evidence for cultural and ethical universals, and thus for "human nature."

Beis points out that had anthropologists done this kind

of work in earlier centuries, things such as the conception of the state of nature as a war of all against all — as described by Thomas Hobbes in *Leviathan*, for example — "would never have been looked on as anything other than a fiction, which in fact, it was." For, as so many anthropologists have pointed out, "anthropological evidence points to the fact that man is by nature a cooperative rather than competitive or aggressive animal." Rousseau's conception of the state of nature "would also receive some hard treatment at the hands of the anthropologists," because the idea that natives lead carefree lives is "a novelistic fiction." Indeed, it is more accurately "the tragic sense of life" that pervades their existence.

Further, Beis argues that living in an age of hyper-relativism ourselves (I add here that the recent so-called postmodernism fad was symptomatic of this), there has nevertheless been a waxing and waning, or flip-flopping, in anthropology studies between belief in universals and belief in relativism. This trend has several identifiable periods. Anthropology as "the study of Man" got off the ground as a "science" as recently as the mid-nineteenth century, and no one then doubted for a moment that there existed something called "Man" to be studied. So from 1860 to 1890, the focus was entirely on elucidation of the "human nature" that was deemed a fact, a constant, and the object of this new "science."

But a certain German named Franz Boas helped change all that. Wishing to escape the anti-Jewish sentiment building in Europe at the time, Boas immigrated to America and ended up heading the newly formed anthropology department of Columbia University. He elaborated a theory of cultural relativism that must be seen in retrospect as an ideological enterprise to defang the sort of absolutism he firmly believed was about to smother Europe, one that he had reason to fear, and one that he believed would always result in totalitarianism.

As a powerful mind and an influential teacher, Boas shaped a couple of generations of American anthropologists who became almost religiously devoted to his relativist ideal. Their teachings dominated the intellectual scene from 1900 to 1945.

Cultural relativism was still very much a force in intellectual circles after the war. But now it was now tempered by the totalitarian experiences of the war itself, and by the dawning realization that people such as Hitler and Mussolini had trumpeted their own versions of ethical relativism as a political ideal *in order to invent their own ethical standards*. Mussolini wrote (this is from my files, not from Beis) that "if relativism signifies contempt for fixed categories and [for] men who claim to be bearers of an external objective truth, *then there is nothing more relativistic than fascist attitudes*" (my italics). Surely there could be no more direct connection between ethical relativism and the totalitarian impulse than those words.

At any rate, Beis goes on to say that from 1945 to "the present" (1964) there was a period of "moderation" among anthropologists who were now driven, by clear human evils, to "reconsider" cultural-relativist positions that had left them without any standard by which to critique human evil or to say that one society is good and another evil. (I add here what Beis could not: I think we are now in a fourth period in which the notion of human universals not only is much more accepted, but also is buttressed by science and technology. Everywhere we turn we see new evidence for biological, genetic, molecular, and brain-based human universals, and these are all deeply spaded new fields, such as evolutionary psychology, cognitive science, neuroscience, and many others.)

Beis then draws up a short list of ethical universals that he extracted from the work of a group of then-famous anthropologists (some of whom had "converted" from their former belief in ethical relativism). It is important to stress here, however, that even though social scientists mostly like to speak of "ethics" rather than of morality, all of the items listed below constitute a kind of international cultural tablet of shared moral norms, standards, and practices meant to guide human behaviour. The cultures sharing these beliefs — all cultures — hold them to be true and to constitute something very close to what some moral philosophers call "exceptionless moral norms."

These are the guiding principles that all people of the world hold to be absolutely true in principle, not relative in the least, and to which practical exceptions may sometimes be acceptable, but only according to special circumstances unforeseeable in the present, to be judged right or wrong when they occur, according to these standards. These moral prohibitions are both self-explanatory and, we might add, self-evidently good, by which I mean that they are aimed at the common good. As such, they require no further explanation. They stand as a rock against the claims of moral and cultural relativists, and my hope is that in future deliberations about morality, the fact and knowledge of their existence will contribute to human solidarity. Here is the professor's list:

1. Prohibition of murder or maiming without justification
2. Prohibition of lying, at least in certain areas such as oaths, etc.
3. Right to own property such as land, clothing, tools, etc.
4. Economic justice: reciprocity and restitution
5. Preference of common good over individual good
6. Demand for co-operation within the group
7. Sexual restriction within all societies
    a) Incest prohibition within nuclear family

b) Prohibition of rape
c) Some form of marriage demanded
d) Prohibition of adultery (with only a few strictly limited legal exceptions)
e) Opposition to promiscuity in the sense of having a large number of partners
f) Lifelong union of the spouses is the ideal
g) Exogamy [marriage outside the family] as a further determination of the incest rule

8. Disrespect for illegitimate children
9. Reciprocal duties between children and parents: parents care for and train children — children respect, obey, and care for parents in old age
10. Loyalty to one's social unit (family, tribe, country)
11. Provision for poor and unfortunate
12. Prohibition of theft
13. Prevention of violence within in-groups
14. Obligation to keep promises
15. Obedience to leaders
16. Respect for the dead and disposal of human remains in some traditional and ritualistic fashion
17. Desire for and priority of immaterial goods [such as knowledge, values, etc.]
18. Obligation to be a good mother
19. Distributive justice
20. Inner rather than external sanctions considered better
21. Courage is a virtue
22. Justice is an obligation

We must conclude, with a feeling of fascination, that all of these ordinances, prohibitions, and standards aimed at the common good, in all human societies for which we have records, evince something like a common human moral nature that seems to be operating as a practical expression of natural law. Otherwise, how is it possible that it is manifested in all people, at all times, in all places, even among people who had no contact with each other? It is this that needs emphasis, celebration, and wonder, and not the myriad differences between us.

CANADA'S SLAVE TRADE

Slavery? In Canada? How could it be? The little booklet *Slavery and Freedom in Niagara*, by Michael Power of Welland, Ontario, got me going on this subject.

In school we learn only that Canada-the-good served as a kind of Holy Land for persecuted slaves who escaped from a barbaric United States. This has created a belief in our moral superiority.

An unjustified belief, for in fact, around the year 1780, there were an estimated four thousand blacks living in the Canadian British colonies, of whom about eighteen hundred were slaves. Canada's first anti-slavery law (of sorts), of July 9, 1793, did not exactly outlaw the practice. It was called "An Act to Prevent the Future Introduction of Slaves." In other words, slavery would remain legal — but no more slaves could be imported to Canada.

Now, it is easy to spring to judgment on all this, until we recall that slavery, practiced at some point prior to this century by almost every known civilization, and defended by Plato and Aristotle as "natural," was until very recently protected by international law. In the eighteenth century, even freedom philosopher John Locke argued that it was morally preferable to the death penalty, which is what many slave captives might otherwise have received. And it is easy to agree that ancient slavery, which was primarily based in the practice of enslaving surrendered enemies who had slaughtered one's own people, was humane (and profitable) compared with slaughtering them in revenge.

Slavery was widely practiced in Africa for millennia by blacks who sold blacks to each other, to Arabs, and to whites. The US census of 1830 records that ten thousand slaves were owned by "free men of colour." Often the first thing a freed slave would do if he got enough money was buy himself a slave. The last nations to outlaw slavery were those on the Arab peninsula, in 1962!

When Columbus arrived in the New World in 1492, he discovered that slavery was already widespread in the local Tiano, Arawak, and Carib tribes, along with cannibalism and torture. Many American and Canadian Indian tribes, such as the Tonkawa of Texas and the Kwakiutl of British Columbia, had been slaveholders (or cannibals, or both) since forever. At the time of white conquest, up to fifteen percent of the Kwakiutl were slaves to their own powerful chiefs. White Europeans arriving in Mexico were horrified to discover that the Aztec civilization was built on slavery, human sacrifice, and the cannibalism of up to two hundred and fifty thousand slaves per year.

As for pioneer Canada, Power writes, "Slave owning was widespread among the emerging political and social elites of Upper Canada." Peter Russell, Matthew Elliot, and many other distinguished men who sat on the Legislative Council of Upper Canada owned dozens of slaves.

Most who owned slaves sought to protect their "right" to do so by arguing that a slave was legally owned property, and the right to own property was basic to all free societies. Courts that took away legally owned slaves could then take away land, or homes, and tyranny would reign.

Farmers asked who would compensate them for their freed slaves, and the lost benefits from slave labour. Many settlers in Upper Canada were Loyalists who had come here because the government had promised them cheap land, on the condition that they cleared it. So slaves were purchased specifically for that purpose. The government had lured the owners of these slaves here. Was the government now going to ruin them?

An irony of the history of slavery in Canada is that many individual US states (Delaware, Michigan, Rhode Island, and Connecticut) had banned slavery outright twenty years before Canada prohibited (only) the future importation of slaves. So the state of Michigan, Power writes, became "an instant haven for slaves escaping from Upper Canada." Canadian slave owners complained bitterly, imploring our Lieutenant-Governor to stop what was in effect a reverse Underground Railroad. He refused.

A friend, exposed to these facts, expressed his instant moral repugnance. "How could they not see the immorality of it?" he asked. My reply was, "Just as we do not see our own." Slaves were legally defined as non-persons, and most people saw that as normal. Future historians will surely wonder at our own tortuous moral and legal chicanery in granting modern mothers the legal "right" to vacuum out — and even crush heads and tear limbs off — young babies in their own wombs. Many of us today see this as normal. This barbaric practice is accepted, and even condoned, because we define unborn humans in our criminal law as non-persons. Ironically, the very same modern liberals who so violently deplore slavery just as violently defend the right to abortion on demand. Like the slave owners of pioneer Canada, they don't see their immorality.

Are we much better off today? Physically, in the sense that we are not owned — yes. But if we ask about control, the answer may be less pleasing. In past times, though less than five percent were slaves, the average citizen, white or black, was quite free of the thousands of meddling laws and controls that deeply invade our persons, property, and privacy — and didn't have to pay a penny of income tax. Yet today entire populations in the "free world" are tax slaves to massive governments for more than half of every year of their lives — and face imprisonment if they refuse to cough up their cash.

Think about it. If you were forced to surrender all your income to government, you would certainly consider yourself a slave. What, then, are you when forced to surrender half your income? Surely the answer is that you are half-enslaved. Ownership of persons is not necessary for a high degree of control. That's why the American revolutionist Josiah Quincy said in 1774 when he cried out against what was then the intolerable idea of taxing human labour: "I speak it with grief — I speak it with anguish — I speak it with shame — I speak it with indignation — we are slaves, the most abject sort of slaves."

HOMELESS? OR FAMILY-LESS?

I confess that I feel a twinge of guilt whenever I pick up my pace to pass a "homeless" man in the streets without giving him some money. But that feeling is mixed with some upset, too — with what might be called civic embarrassment. I ask myself why our wealthy modern societies have increasing numbers of people whom we choose to call "homeless." That word is in quotes because it is a public euphemism meant to divert our attention from a deeper underlying truth, which is that most of these people are not so much "homeless" as family-less. Many are so shiftless, drunk, high, aimless, or irresponsible (or some combination of these things) that their own families want nothing more to do with them. Many of them have turned their backs on their families and homes themselves, tired of all the advice to get a job.

To use the word "homeless" is to fall into a lazy way of thinking that glosses over a far deeper situation.

Toronto recently spent $90,000 on a survey of the "homeless," the results of which will tell us nothing new. The many socialists working away at tax-funded jobs will use the study to proclaim the need for more "resources" and more "shelters" and more "housing" for these unfortunates. But what is the true relationship between the increasing numbers of "homeless" and the rest of us? Why, for some four decades now, have we been seeing more helpless, needy people sleeping in our streets, splayed dead drunk or high as kites over subway grates, pissing themselves in public, panhandling, or worst of all, freezing to death in winter?

It's a long story. But part of what disturbs me is the idea that many of these unfortunate people are ideological victims of a trend that started in the 1960s. That was when as students we were exposed to the "revolutionary" thinking of the "anti-psychiatry" movement. Now, it is true that psychiatry is something that bears watching. By the middle of the last century, so many citizens were shoved into mental institutions against their will, under the authority of any number of "writs of involuntary commitment," that it began to seem like the whole of society might eventually be locked up. In 1962 the famous Midtown Manhattan Study had declared that eighty percent of the population of Manhattan was "psychiatrically impaired," and twenty-three percent so severely as to require immediate treatment. And never mind the abuses by angry people wanting to declare their rich relatives insane and loot their estates, and the like.

However, the 1960s were a time for liberation from all sorts of constraints, and psychiatry and the abuses of involuntary commitment quickly became a target. In a strange intellectual liaison, libertarian anti-psychiatrists like Dr. Thomas Szasz found themselves allied with leftists and strident Marxists like Herbert Marcuse, R.D. Laing, and the French sociologist Michel Foucault. Books such as Laing's *The Politics of the Family*, Szasz's *The Myth of Mental Illness*, and Foucault's *Madness and Civilization* all sang the same song. "Madness" is not something real, the lyrics went; it is defined by the powerful and serves as a political instrument to remove weak and undesirable people from public view via incarceration. In fact, they argued, it is bourgeois capitalist society that is mad, and so-called madness in individuals is actually an appropriate reaction, a coping device of sorts, in a world that is itself crazy.

By the same token, Laing (who later recanted) argued infamously that a lot of madness was a "sane" reaction to the insanity of oppressive family dynamics. All of them denied that madness has any organic basis in body chemistry or the brain (now dramatically disproved by miracle drugs that help normalize life for so many) and described it as a "social construction" — a mythical condition made up to justify political and social motives such as removing unpleasantness from the streets (or, in the case of the USSR, of removing political enemies), and to justify treatment by mental health experts hungry for more patients.

Of course, there was a good deal of truth to all this. But then there was overreaction and overcorrection. The result was that governments seeking to save costs, and libertarians and Marxists critical of society for different reasons, found themselves colluding to end not just some but all writs of involuntary confinement. And so by the 1970s the insane asylums of the Western world began to empty.

By the 1980s the rather disturbing public result was written up by Rael Jean Isaac and Virginia C. Armat, in their excellent study *Madness in the Streets: How Psychiatry and the Law Abandoned the Mentally Ill*. These authors, as have many since, cite copious evidence that some thirty-five to fifty percent of all "homeless" people are in fact, by any reasonable measure, mentally ill, and they argue that the post-1960s liberation movement that has ejected them from mental hospitals onto the street is cruel and has done them a great disservice.

Think about it. If public authorities are told of a man in the street with a broken leg, you will hear the fire engines and ambulances coming from miles away. But if they are told of a man in the street with a broken mind, you will hear only silence. In other words, the new freedom for the mentally ill is in fact a new form of punishment, and if the weather is cold enough, it may also be a sentence by an uncaring society of execution.

A Hero Gone

"Sorry for your loss," a friend told me last week.

This was said about a quiet, taciturn man whose recent death at seventy-four from pancreatic cancer struck me surprisingly hard. I felt this man's death as something quite personal, even though I had not seen him for some twenty years. I wondered why his passing was such a blow. I concluded that though he was not a close friend, he had somehow settled into my psyche as a sporting hero. It was as if, with his death, some of the familiar and comforting furniture of my life had been carried away without warning.

He was a leathery-faced, kindly man named Kauko Riihiaho. It took some work to get him laughing, but then came the twinkle, and then the genuine mirth. He was a carpenter by trade, who came to Canada with his family in the 1960s from Finland, where, as National Junior Champion in cross-country skiing, he left behind him a reputation akin to that of hockey's Wayne Gretzky in Canada.

So it was fitting that I first met him on the snow. It was at my Dad's farm, in 1973. A few of us beginners had gathered, new skis in hand, excited to try a freshly made 1.3-kilometer track through winding bush. This was old-style, single-track skiing, for which you had better interpret the topography well before each push of the skis or risk losing a lot of time. There was a lovely and intimate fluffy whiteness to be enjoyed, gliding past pine branches that spilled cold snow on your heated body. As a former Olympic athlete and only thirty-three, I figured I was strong enough to master this new sport pretty quickly. So we asked Kauko to show us how it was done.

We were soon treated to the sight of true athletic grace as he glided effortlessly along, everything in a perfect natural rhythm, even up the hills, while we slipped and thrashed, way behind him. The best we could manage, pushing hard, was about seven minutes a loop, and two or three times around was a tough workout. So, the lesson over and our bodies tired, we agreed to go in for some hearty soup.

"Kauko, are you coming?"

"No thank you," he said in halting English. "Now I go for ski."

"Huh? We were just skiing. How long will you stay out?"

"Maybe two hour."

We were astonished at the mere idea, so we hung around a bit to watch him. How long would each loop take him, unencumbered by his acolytes? Well, he ticked by us twice at a steady pace of four and a-half minutes, and that's when the awe and hero-worship began.

In the decade that followed, when a two- or three-hour hard ski had become normal even for us, we raced against him on many occasions. All of us remember thirty-kilometer races when we felt that because we were now doing *so* well, and were much younger than he, and had started a full fifteen minutes earlier than he ... that just maybe this time we wouldn't see him before the finish. But inevitably we would soon hear the regular "snick-snick-snick" of his poles in the snow, and maybe a little exertion-cough just to let us know he was about to run us down, and then the mumbled word "track" to get us out of the way so he could pass fast, always looking so very fine, balanced on one ski, his other leg kicking like a mule. We had heard that anyone who refused to move over for him might feel the tips of his ski poles in their lower back as he took care of that for them (though I never saw him do this).

In a race he was definitely a man on a mission. For a half-minute or so after he went by, we would try to keep up, shaking our heads at how, despite our best efforts, he just kept moving relentlessly away from us. Cross-country grip waxes are rated for temperature, and if you use a wax rated colder than the snow you are on, you will just slip and get horribly frustrated. All his competitive life Kauko used grip waxes at least one, maybe two, grades colder than other racers. I know people who raced against him when he was on the Canadian National team who still say, "We all thought he had some secret recipe. No one ever figured out how he did it." Mostly, it was technique; he didn't need grippy wax like the rest of us. He was a snow dancer, weighting each ski just exactly right, fully, and at the right time.

After a race, standing around a bonfire deep in the woods, stripping off damp shirts without a thought at -20C, and having some beer, he and his equally tough older Finnish friends, some of whom had fought against the Russian invaders in World War II, would tell stories about being on a Finnish ski patrol, armed and dangerous. Covered in white make-up, rifles on their backs, a half-dozen of them would ski together, guided only by compasses (no walkie-talkies allowed), over frozen rolling hills at dusk, searching out disabled Russian trains, It was the most continuously cold winter in Finnish history — never above minus thirty degrees for three months.

When these killers in white neared a convoy halted by the bitter cold, they would fall forward and lie on their skis, gripping the tips with their hands. Then they would shuffle forward in the deep snow, slowly and carefully, a few feet at a time. The Russian sentries were posted about a hundred meters apart; shuffle too vigorously, and they would wheel and shoot you dead in the snow.

Then, within range and at the right moment, the Finns would reach for their rifles (Kauko said the best marksmen could put a bullet in a man's eye at a hundred metres) and shoot the enemy in the back.

Mission accomplished, they would leave quickly, and then: "We ski about thirty kilometer more to next convoy. And shoot again." The Russians, who had clodhopper skis and no waxes at all, had no hope of chasing them down, so fast were the Finns, even through unbroken snow. "Russians think we have few dozen patrol in different places. But it was only us, moving fast."

This amazed us all, and we asked: "After skiing so far to attack again, in such cold, how did you get dry? Where did you sleep?"

"We ski one more hour, slow, to dry off, then with special blanket, go under snow like dog, to sleep a little."

One older friend said that he didn't go inside a human habitation for almost three months during that famous winter war.

Kauko and his other Finnish ski friends were all tough like that, whether skiing, orienteering, or running like deer through the bush. We admired them for their uncomplaining fortitude. Training with them, we could actually feel a little of it rubbing off now and then, making us feel like manlier men. It was their gift to us.

Can There Be Morality on the Moon?

At a recent conference I got embroiled in arguments after making the statement that the term "morality" has no meaning if we are utterly alone — that it only takes on a meaning when there is at least one more person present, because only then may our behaviour affect someone else, for better or worse, and, reciprocally, may our conduct be judged by others, rather than just by ourselves.

This really threw the cat amongst the pigeons. A couple of doctrinaire libertarians immediately took the floor to reject my position. "How can you say such a thing? Individual morality is the basis of society!"

I have lots of libertarian (pro-freedom-of-the-individual) instincts myself, I replied, and the individualism behind it sounds good at first. But if we reflect more deeply, it becomes clear that the word "morality" makes no sense in the context of true solitude. For when our actions concern only ourselves, they are neither moral nor immoral — they are just preferences, choices, tastes, or passions that we indulge or reject.

By now I was feeling the heat, because this example threatens the popular Western notion of morality according to which we believe we can act as our own morality-judges. ("You do your thing, and I'll do mine," or "It's true for you, but it's not true for me," and so on.)

Until very recently, however, people have always understood that we are social beings who live together inside a kind of public moral bubble that covers the entire community. Each of us freely participates in the creation — or destruction — of the moral standards inside the bubble through our beliefs, opinions, and daily actions concerning the ultimate issues of life. So much has this been so for most of human history that even in the early days of modern democracy, there was not much doubt that a majority vote would also be the public moral vote. Then, the people as a whole were considered a kind of jury. But it was not long before those two things — majorities, and a fragmenting morality — began to wander off in different directions. Communities weakened.

Those who had proudly defended themselves against the raw power of the state soon also began to defend against the moral opinions of society at large; that is, against whatever moral opinion was inside the bubble. "Don't tell me how to behave," was the new rallying call. It wasn't long before people wanted outside the bubble altogether. They each wanted a bubble of their own. Of course, all this simply strengthened the state while weakening the bonds of society, which has always been the best protector of the individual against the state.

At any rate, this new idea soon found its prophet in John Stuart Mill, and by the latter half of the nineteenth century the rather peculiar idea had arisen (dignified by Mill's little 1859 booklet *On Liberty*) that to be free and happy, each of us should conceive of ourselves as living according to our private wishes. Our bubbles need never collide unless we do something to harm someone else, or they harm us. What constitutes harm in such a system is a much larger question, and in the latter part of his booklet — which even today few ever read — Mill himself specified so many qualifications and limits regarding what is individually good or bad behaviour that he pretty much undid all his earlier defences of the individual bubble idea.

Despite these weaknesses, and for some reason that is

now unclear, but that may be understood by future historians, moral theory in the Western world came to more or less wholly embrace Mill's simple individual-bubble idea (likely because it is so simple).

It is the contradictions in this incoherent theory that interest me the most. Perhaps an example will illustrate these best.

Let us suppose that you find yourself utterly alone on the moon. You have sufficient supplies to survive but clearly are flying solo for the rest of your life. My claim is that, try as you may, you cannot do anything "moral" or "immoral," because no one except you can evaluate your actions. For example, you may decide to use a drug that was illegal back on Earth, or to shout some forbidden "hate speech" as loud as possible over the barren moonscape. But aside from some kind of residual shame or guilt brought with you from Earth, there is no one else with respect to whom these actions can be said to be moral or immoral.

My wife objected that she would nonetheless feel like a regular moral being alone on the moon, because she would still be accountable to God. That was a pretty good argument. So I thought about her reply and answered that for Christians like her, God is a personal God (everywhere felt, nowhere seen), and so she cannot really say she is ever alone.

A conference participant who all but verbally accosted me the next morning called me "a collectivist" for my views. We all have "a personal moral code," he spluttered (this was a variation of the individual bubble theory), and so we can behave morally or immorally with respect to that code all by ourselves. (I think his personal code was a stand-in for his god, or for the missing "other.") You are speaking like a collectivist, he insisted, because you want to impose a group morality on me!

I responded that he was dead wrong on two counts. First, he had chosen the wrong word, because true collectivists have a monopoly on force, so anything they do is the farthest thing from morality. Second, my example of the public moral bubble was not collectivist because it is a matter of free participation by all adults, and not coercion. We will all naturally feel a strong moral pressure when we understand the shalls and shall-nots inside the bubble, but we freely abide by or reject them and pay the price or reap the reward accordingly.

But alone on the moon (without a code-companion, or God watching), morality is a non-issue, because there is no one to help or harm except yourself, and you are the only judge of that. That is why (likely as a historical recognition of this truth), the most famous universal caveat on human behaviour is that "No one can be a judge in his own case." That is why I say that morality is not possible on the moon, because if you were alone, you would be making — and remaking, or breaking — the rules of a code that you made up to suit only yourself; there would be only a play-judge, because no one can act as a legislator and a judge of himself at the same time (that this can be done is one of Mill's false assumptions). Such an attempt can only produce a dialogue of the deaf between two conflicting aspects (one a ruler, the other the ruled) of the same personality — you! Indeed, without the possibility of impartial judgment of our behaviour (by others acting according to some shared and publicly accepted standard of conduct, which no single individual has invented), morality can have neither force nor effect, and therefore has no real meaning other than the vanity of self-satisfaction. (Today I will try my best to do what I said yesterday I would do.)

A good parallel for this reality is human language. We all speak according to rules that none of us individually has invented and that none of us can alter by ourselves. In effect, Mill's individual moral bubble theory is a way of placing each of us on a private moon, with a private language. In terms of a shared sense of the good and the bad, his view has been a disaster for the West, because it produces a rudderless social ship: all the passengers wander about as they please, with no common course in mind, drifting.

One of Mill's most stringent critics at the time, James Stephens, complained that the personal bubble idea would eventually destroy every system of morals, for it conceived of human beings as a pack of hounds, all chained together, but always straining to go in different directions. To be fair, it was only during the period of what I call his "liberty outburst" that Mill thought all this was just fine. For most of his life he insisted that the self must be subordinate to the common good and subject to a "restraining influence." There are, he declared, "fundamental principles" that men hold sacred and that are "above discussion," and without which there is a natural tendency to anarchy. Stephens agreed, of course, and in a memorable turn of phrase remarked that a parliamentary government is just such a system of mild public restraint, whereby in order to live well together, we agree in advance to count heads instead of breaking them.

But alas, today, because we no longer agree on basic terms such as right and wrong public conduct, we fight a lot, and when, as they must, our miserable little bubbles collide and we can no longer settle things between ourselves, we are driven by frustration to sue each other and run to judges, charters, tribunals, and the like to arbitrate our conflicts.

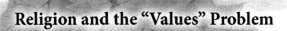

II

Religion and the "Values" Problem

On Atheism

A University of Toronto student group calling itself the Toronto Secular Alliance has demanded that the university eliminate a prayer to "Eternal God" that is used at its annual spring graduation ceremony, on the grounds that such prayers exclude atheists. Surely, goes the argument, such ceremonies ought to be "inclusive." The ceremony has included a prayer since it was first held in 1827, and only in 1990 changed the words "Eternal Father" to "Eternal God." There is more here than meets the eye.

My own formative years were spent at Appleby College in Oakville, Ontario, then a Protestant school, the headmaster of which was a formidable man. The routine was chapel for twenty minutes every morning, group prayers at night before bed, and church Sunday morning in Oakville and again Sunday evening back at the school. I was a choir boy and soloist, and I am still deeply moved by all the religious music we sang: Bach, Handel, Mozart's *Ave Verum*, and so many other great works. Although ten years ago I decided to read the New Testament very closely, I don't go to church much any more, and I describe myself as a disappointed Anglican. The last time I went to church, the minister harangued us about being good citizens, urging us to use our Blue Boxes for recycling. I figured he should have been talking about the garbage in our souls instead of the garbage on our streets.

What bothers me in debates about religion is the absence of rigorous logic, the unwillingness to budge, and the failure to be awed by the mere fact of existence. So here are a few thoughts on religion and faith positions.

I was once a cocky atheist myself, so I have a feeling for where all this is "coming from," as they say. So now, whenever I hear a committed atheist say triumphantly, "I don't believe in God," I immediately ask, "How did you come by your faith?" After a bit of a stunned silence, and often also with a bit of a self-confident smirk, the fellow then says, "What do you mean, 'my faith'? I just said I don't believe in God!"

To which I reply (and at this point I anticipate a certain quizzical look): "Well, I believe in God, but I can't prove he exists. And you don't believe in God, and you can't prove he doesn't exist. So my point is that we are both arguing from a faith position. So now what I want to know is how did you come by your faith?"

By now he is a little upset.

"Well," I go on, "I think life itself is pretty close to a miraculous thing, and I have no natural explanation for it or for the universe itself, other than that it must have been the work of some almighty power, the direct knowledge of which I am denied by my inadequate nature. That is my faith position.

"You, on the other hand — I have heard you say this before — believe that the universe created itself from nothing, even though you cannot explain how something comes from nothing, and that life also created itself through some kind of chemical or biological necessity, which you cannot demonstrate either. It's all faith. And furthermore, I think that it is far more bizarre to believe that all sorts of miraculous things that we cannot explain or replicate, from the incredible complexity of the single cell to our vast cosmos, simply sprang into being one day by themselves for no reason whatsoever, than to believe they were caused by some almighty agent. I understand why you call my faith primitive, and so on. But yours seems to me even worse — it is a belief in magic. At least I propose a *possible* cause, whereas when I ask you about causes, you just feed me mumbo-jumbo about mathematical "singularities" in physics, and "prebiotic soup."

"You cannot even explain the difference between your own brain and your mind," I say.

To my dialogue partner's objection to that, I say: "Yes, the very instrument you are using to think, your brain, is a solid thing. But all day long it produces non-things that we call ideas and feelings (what contemporary philosophers of mind call *qualia*, or qualities). Now tell me, how can a thing produce a non-thing? If I say lift your little finger, and you do so, how is that possible? 'It's a nerve impulse travelling from my brain to my finger, at so-and-so miles per hour,' you say.

"But does the 'nerve' simply decide to get up and travel? Or was it told to travel? And if so, what told it to do so? Was it another impulse? If you say yes, I deny that this is possible on the grounds that a material thing cannot motivate another material thing to do anything. So it must have got started by a non-thing. In this case, by your will, which, you must agree, is immaterial. It's the same with all existence."

And then we go drink some beer together.

A Machine-gun Conversion

Jimmy, a black American taxi driver with whom I once spent an hour in Colorado Springs, told me a harrowing story of his time spent in a US gunboat in Vietnam. He said the whole damn boat, with its 1.5-inch steel cladding, and four or five macho, football-player type, cocky atheists like him inside, was drifting down this misty river, looking for Vietcong "gooks," or a stray animal — anything on which they could practise their shooting. A happy, bloodthirsty, only slightly nervous pack of weed-smoking studs.

Suddenly, all hell broke loose. The explosions were so loud, his hearing was damaged for life. Smoke filled the boat; enormous shells tore through that steel armour like it was paper, and one of them went right through the heart of his best friend as they were talking, eyeball to eyeball, and left a hole Jimmy said he could have put his fist through. The rest lived to tell about it, although three of them were terribly maimed.

Jimmy was lucky. But he said he will never forget that the only words he heard, in the midst of all the shouting and blood-splattered panic, and the *boom-boom* of return machine-gun fire, words cried with a visceral, tangible pleading so deep it shook him for the rest of his life: "Oh God, I don't wanna die," "Oh God, please help me," followed by "Mama, Mama," and "Mom, Mom! Help me, help me, please!" These hulking 230-pound linebackers were calling for God and their mothers.

Jimmy became a believer in that moment. He saw my upcoming reaction: Of course. You were frightened, so you were reaching for security. No, he insisted, his conversion was not due to his own chicken-hearted panic (of which he'd had aplenty). He was not "an atheist in a foxhole," he insisted. This was not some insight he could have come to on his own, a thing that he willed, but something that happened to him, invaded his whole being, from outside and despite himself. Prior to that moment, he figured he had been pretty happy as a card-carrying atheist, like so many of his friends. They had talked that way cruising down the river, looking for someone to kill.

He had been changed, not by any direct contact with God (as far as he could tell), or even by the terrible vaporization of his closest friend, which he could never forget, but by a primordial truth that I figure was delivered by raw experience. The protective bravado and pretence of their lives had suddenly blown up, and just as suddenly they were in intimate contact with each other as the mournful, beseeching, and disembodied souls which that instant revealed them to be — something he now knew with an indelible certainty they really, truly were.

If you survive such an experience, Jimmy said, "if you receive the gift of life," you can never go back to believing only in yourself. And you can never, never forget. And I will never forget his story.

Opus Dei and "No Pain, No Gain"

The other night the CBC ran a special about Opus Dei, the Catholic organization now famous because of the role attributed to it in the bestselling novel *The Da Vinci Code.* I have not read this book and will probably not see the movie, even though intimates inform me that it is a rousing tale of the potboiler type. The CBC was making an effort to appear understanding, but the simple fact of presenting such a topic on national television presupposes criticism. We saw and heard a pleasant member of Opus Dei explain how he wears an uncomfortable spiked chain around his leg for two hours a week, and periodically whips himself on the butt with a toy whip — all this in the hope of sharing the suffering and pain of his hero and saviour, Jesus Christ. Indeed, he is hoping that in imitating Christ, some of the spiritual closeness will rub off. He believes that his hero must have felt just like this, so this is what it feels like to be him.

Is this weird? Well, I'm pretty sure that despite its strained neutrality on this topic, our national network once again saw itself as playing a crucial role in showing us that religion, especially Catholicism is, um, very retro. The message that came through was that self-inflicted pain, or "self-mortification," is weird (and therefore religion is weird).

Now I am not certain of the meaning of self-mortification, but I suspect it has something to do with dying to yourself, or making your own physical self die, so to speak, so that your spirit can be free from the bonds, allurements, pleasures, and deceptions of the flesh. The underlying notion is that the spirit is always threatened with enslavement to the body.

This reminds me that most of the key writings in our tradition document a struggle in which central figures attempt either to lose the self through immersion in bodily pleasure, or to escape the body and its appetites altogether in search of a purely spiritual experience. For the former type, intense pleasure is the road to ecstasy. There is even a drug called Ecstasy that serves this purpose. I believe that the word is rooted in *ex-stasis* — to exit from the static, or from what is, or from ordinary bodily life and awareness. At any rate, this type escapes the self through physical enjoyment. For the latter type, mortification, or physical pain, is the proper route to ecstasy.

How common are these two methods of escaping the self today? And is there a sense in which not just Opus Dei members, but our entire civilization, is caught up in one or the other of them?

It is quite possible that the CBC interviewer, perhaps a confirmed secularist, left the studio feeling gratified that he had exposed religion as a weird self-punishment thing, then happily strapped on his jogging shoes and ran a very painful ten kilometers to make himself feel purified and "fit," or to get "an endorphin high." There are millions of people, and I am one of them, who make a daily habit of this sort of self-mortification.

I am absolutely certain that two hours a week of whipping your butt with a toy whip to feel better spiritually is no match for a two-hour ride over punishing hills with my son. I mean, we really grind it out. There is intense pain in the thighs, burning lungs, lactic acid in the mouth, and stiffness that can last for days. And sometimes we wear that yellow bracelet, or even a special Lance Armstrong biking shirt … and we imagine for a moment, on the crest of a hill, that this is what it must feel like to be him.

And when I go to the gym, I see hundreds of people, blood vessels bulging, pumping huge machines; assuming horribly twisted and painful poses in their Yoga classes; donning boxing gloves and slugging the hell out of each other; suffering broken hands, ribs, or feet in smelly karate classes; or even — I have witnessed it — losing an eye to a squash ball. Fitness and sport are popular forms of ecstasy that we are convinced lift us above or out of ordinary life. Hundreds of millions of people daily drive themselves through this experience of reaching for a feeling of emotional or spiritual purity — even, admittedly, a kind of superiority to other human beings — all because of the pain they are willing to take. Those of us who number among them say, "No pain, no gain." Coaches all over the globe tell their athletes, "Go hard, or go home," meaning, if it doesn't hurt, you're not pushing yourself hard enough.

And on it goes. Afterward we often get into a popular form of ecstasy called beer, or booze, and many of us suffer the painful consequences the next morning. Some people slowly kill themselves this way. During the day I see women suffering voluntary pain for hours at a time in high heels, all for the pleasure of personal vanity. In my own case, all my physical pains — a broken and now disabled shoulder joint (three surgeries) and back surgery ten years ago (from an old long-jumping injury) — give me pain for a lot more than two hours a day, often even waking me at night. But I don't regret a thing. It was all for the glory and the high of sports that I have loved.

So it's not just Opus Dei members who practise self-mortification. Maybe the CBC should do a little corrective programming about just how normal this is.

BABY SEALS AND BABIES

I never thought that ex-Beatle Sir Paul McCartney had much of a voice. Now I wonder about his morals. Not that he doesn't have any. Obviously he does. He is eager to let us know what a sensitive fellow he is. There he was, stretched out on the endless whiteness of a Canadian ice floe, his wife alongside, trying to pet a cute baby seal for the cameras. Sir Paul's humanitarian message was that all human beings should be deeply moved by the killing of even a single baby … seal.

The week before this photo op, a Chinese woman was in all the papers, vilified by the whole animal-loving world for taking pleasure in killing baby cats. It seems that she makes videos of herself petting little kittens and then slowly and meticulously crushing their heads under her heel. She sees it as performance art, where the goal is to be able to do such things without showing any feeling, turning her into a true artist. The Internet and media community experienced instant outrage over this intentionally vile act of cruelty. The message was that we ought to be deeply moved by the killing of even a single baby … kitten.

I don't get it. Where is the outrage about the killing of a cute baby … human?

I promise not to exaggerate. I am just asking a question. Why have we never seen a photo of Sir Paul in a Canadian hospital reaching out with heart-rending sympathy to touch the nose of a freshly aborted human baby? Or perhaps laying his head on the rounded belly of the mother, just before the act of bloody extraction, his tears trickling onto the sheet as the cameras grind?

I know, I know. Most human baby-killing is in the first trimester. They are, well, not recognizably human yet. Not like the cute little seal or the meowing kitten. I can hear it now: "Don't play that game, buddy. This is about stuff that *can really move you!*" Okay, okay. But the human heart does start beating in the womb at twenty-one days. And the entire genetic endowment specific to each and every individual human baby — just like the baby seal's and the kitten's genetic endowment — is there at conception. I mean, I'm just having a little trouble with *the value thing.* About why the seal and the kitten rate so high with Sir Paul and the public, but human babies are off the radar screen.

Sir Paul even told Larry King that sealing is exactly like the ancient slave trade, that it is a barbaric practice that continues without justification. So I find myself substituting just a couple of words for his, wondering how the world would have reacted if he had told Larry King, "Killing unborn baby humans is like the ancient slave trade, and a barbaric practice that continues without justification."

Most people are unaware that somewhere around two to three percent of all Canadian and American abortions occur in the third trimester. These are definitely baby human beings. I didn't say "persons." Good heavens. Calling a human being a "person" without legal permission, that is, before it is fully born could get me put in jail for a hate crime. The Supreme Courts of both Canada and the US say that a human being is not a person until it leaves the womb alive. No lie. It's called the "born-alive" rule. But they didn't say it wasn't a *human being,* or that it is not *human life.* Obviously it is not a baby seal, or a kitten. And maybe, in the public mind, it's not as cute as those. But the rule has caused some inconveniences that ought to attract Sir Paul's attention.

About a hundred and twenty-five thousand baby human lives are taken in Canada each year and over a million and a quarter annually in the US. An unknown number of these third-trimester babies in the US and Europe are killed by "partial-birth abortion." This technique is prohibited in Canada, so far, but not in the US where former President Bill Clinton refused to sign a law prohibiting it. And anyway, unlike for baby seals, it is not as if government inspectors are watching over abortion clinics to make sure that human babies are killed "humanely."

The inconvenience of the born-alive rule is that third-trimester babies are very large — at least as large as baby seals. Many second-trimester babies are killed and then dismembered in the womb. Pulled out an arm and a leg at a time. That is routine. Whatever. But it's a tough assignment if there is a large kid inside. The abortionist sure doesn't want to go to jail for killing a "person." So to make extraction easier and to remain inside the law, he turns the baby around in the womb and drags it out by the feet until just the head remains inside the mother. Then, with a sharp instrument — usually a pair of scissors — he punches a hole in the back of the baby's head (the baby flexes, as if he is falling) and with a small vacuum hose sucks out the brains so that the skull will collapse and he can drag the kid out easily. Not born alive. And so — we are asked to believe — not yet a person. And certainly not a baby seal. But it sure looks like a human being to me. So I still don't get it.

III

Sex, Women, and Family

WOMEN AND MONEY

Egalitarians, with a boost from Statistics Canada, are all in a lather over the fact that women are "losing the battle of the sexes" in terms of their "earning power." We are informed that too many of them — sixty-seven percent — prefer the "pink ghetto" to the boardroom, the same percentage as a decade ago, and that the level of female managers (oh, the national shame of it!) has "dropped back" to where it was two decades ago. So we are said to be "losing the war for general equality."

Statistics Canada is surprised, in light of the higher number of educated women today, by "the continuing stubborn wage gap," and by the number of women still working in traditionally female jobs.

A little voice asks: What if women *prefer* the so-called pink ghetto? And anyway, who says women and men must crave the same jobs, and earn the same pay? *Never-married women and never-married men in Canada have always earned about the same wages.* Actually, the last time I investigated this ridiculous battle of the sexes, a couple of decades were shown in which never-married women earned *more* than never-married men. Fact is, the great majority of healthy women not already brainwashed by a materialistic, commercial society do not crave money and job status. They do not want the boardroom. They want a strong male earner in the bedroom. And from him they want healthy, beautiful babies, a happy family, and a financially secure life. That is what they have craved since they were teenagers. Some of them get it. But far too few.

Statistics Canada's own figures on the earnings of never-married women show that what causes the "wage gap" is the natural female preference for marriage and children over commercial work outside the home. Mothers refuse jobs that are too demanding or switch to part-time work, so they can fulfill their own ambition to raise their kids properly. Some cannot afford to turn money down, however, and it is a national scandal that millions of them have become wage dupes of a modern welfare state that so badly needs their tax dollars. Such states strive to keep as many men and women in the workforce as possible, paying as much in taxes as possible, so the state can take over as much of life's most meaningful functions as possible, such as child-rearing in government daycare centres, education in government schools, social welfare needs in government housing and programs, and care of the sick in government-controlled hospitals and old-age homes.

Don't buy it. Fight it. If the good wife really wants to work outside the home, fine. But be aware that millions of women are trapped there. And, in addition to very high taxes that suppress the standard of living, what traps them is our very strange public attitude about equality, whereby we insist on making different things — such as men and women — the same in all ways even though they are by nature different in most ways. So I say, instead of falling for such a transparent ruse, let's encourage as many men as possible to be real men, take better jobs, work harder, and go for pay raises to get their wives out of the work force and raising their own kids at home. Shame on Statistics Canada for participating in this number-juggling scam.

GRIEVING NICHOLA

When I first heard the news, I was shocked and felt a tangible grieving for Nichola Goddard, the first Canadian woman ever to die fighting in battle. For some reason it struck me as more than the death of someone who was clearly a wonderful person and a highly capable soldier. Like most Canadians, I am intensely proud of her and the life she gave up for me, my family, my children, and my people. She is a hero in my mind. Nevertheless, I will always believe that no matter how good women may be as soldiers, sending them to battle in place of men is wrong. And the fact that we do will always make me feel a little guilty and even shamed, as a man. I can't help that. It is what I feel, and deeply so.

But how can it make sense to be so proud of her soldiering, yet so upset that we sent her off to die?

Call this the knee-jerk, dinosaur emotion of an unrepentant male reactionary, if you like. But I ask, how can it be right for a country filled with strong and vital men to send women into battle to die in their place? In their place, you say? She chose that life! She loved what she was doing! True. But while an individual's choice of something, if it is good, makes it good for that person, it does not follow that such a choice is good or right or best for society as a whole.

Why do I and so many others feel this way? Why has every Canadian man worth the name felt an inner twinge of conscience over her death?

Well, for starters, women have a unique role in society that men can never fill: they give birth to other human beings and nurture human life in ways that men cannot. All men know that. And most men grow up with an inbred awe of, and respect for, that natural fact of life. That is, we have the intuitive knowledge that civilization would come to a grinding halt if women, the mothers of us all, died out. So, it seems to a man (again so strongly and intuitively) that although it is a noble tragedy for a nation to lose a single life in battle, it is a kind of double tragedy to lose a woman's life. For a young woman who dies in battle loses her own life and also the lives for which she was a living proxy-in-waiting.

This is the deepest mystery of the female, and it is why losing a woman in war is rightly felt as so costly to all. Fighting men know this in their hearts, and to deny this truth is to oppose what is sometimes called the life force, and therefore to rend the very fabric of society.

For just as there is nothing higher or nobler for women than to create human life and nurture it, so there is nothing nobler for men than to love and protect their women and children, and if necessary to die for them. All manly men feel this call deeply. It is strange to say, perhaps, and against all common sense, but many men love war precisely because it gives them the opportunity to be heroic, to be altruistic, to answer a higher calling of a kind that all women feel naturally in creating life — a calling that is not natural or available to men in this biological and instinctive way. So deeply do most men need and long for this that they will unhesitatingly face terrible odds in battle and willingly die to protect their fellows. Call it a guy thing. But this is why I say there is something deeply amiss with the values of our society when a Nichola is killed, and the same day back home a few hundred thousand very tough men go to work, play their sports, go out at night to drink and dance, and then go home for a good sleep.

It is the truth of this stark contrast that hit the manliness of our country as a whole like a body blow. For just as it would be wrong and cowardly, and would instantly and naturally incur loathing in any manly man, to watch another man beat up a woman for the last space on a lifeboat, so it is wrong and incurs a silent shame in most men to see women go to battle in their place. Especially against a Muslim enemy that they know is outraged to be fighting against women in the first place and so is very eager to target them first. And what real man would argue that if we had two platoons of Canadian soldiers, one all-female, and one all-male, both equally prepared to attack the enemy, that it would be right or natural to send the women's platoon in first? None. That would go against nature and against the deepest male instinct and desire to fight and protect.

For these reasons I fear that we are putting women at risk in war to satisfy a strangely powerful but misguided ideological craving for equality in all things. Indeed, it seems that we crave such equality in inverse proportion to our loss of confidence in the great and natural truths of human life. So strong is this pathetic and very recent public ideal that we now demand that all things male and female that are clearly and naturally different must be officially denied and made the same at all costs. We are prepared to fudge the truth and to change all social reality to make them so.

Nichola died for her country. But she also died, whether she knew it or not, in the name of a stridently radical ideology that has been weakening the social and family fabric of Canada for more than three decades, and in the name of which she got to the front lines. She chose this because it was available. And it fulfilled her as an individual. So we have to believe she died happy. But as a society, it is we who chose to make that choice possible for her. I just don't think that any life, male or female, should be sacrificed to an ideal so clearly wrong-headed and against natural truth.

There Can Be No Sex in Homosexual

Has anyone noticed that our endless public wrangling over political and legal rights has mostly to do with the human body? Surely this indicates that something very important has changed.

The central moral preoccupations and concerns of robust civilizations have always been about the great mysteries of human existence, such as knowing the will of God, the nature of destiny and fate, the ultimate meaning of the cosmos, the quality of the common good, how to imbue children with virtue, prudence, courage, and justice, and so on.

But today we simply assume that all that minor stuff has been squared away forever, and so now, as enlightened and liberated folk, we are free to argue about our personal appetites and desires. But whether speaking of marriage, homosexuality, abortion, euthanasia, swinging, or divorce, we are basically fighting in a confused way about the body and its functions, and all of this started with confusions of language.

Orwell said that words are like harpoons: once you get them in, it's hard to get them out. And certainly, those who wish to dissolve traditional society have been very good at getting the rest of us to use their words. For example, we all use the term "pro-choice" rather than "pro-abortion," which is the truer description of that position. And when we speak of euthanasia we say we are "helping" a sick person die, instead of "making" them die.

In a recent lead *National Post* editorial about lowering the age of consent, we had to endure a lecture about "sexual" equality for gays and lesbians and "the nature of their sexual relationship." If the editors of the *Post* are going to invoke the word "nature," then maybe they ought to follow through naturally.

I mean to say, if this discussion is to proceed beyond the infantile clamouring for equality of rights by which it is now characterized — if we want to properly discuss such things in full possession of the proper terms of debate — then we have to examine more precisely the words we use.

So here is my opening try.

"Sex" is a biological term, and biologists and life scientists all over the world use the words "sex" or "sexual" only with reference to plant or animal behaviour that has a reproductive potential. To use such words in connection with the behaviour of entities that cannot or do not (or choose not to) reproduce together, is either dumb, sloppy, or intentionally political (or all of these at once).

There are lots of animals and humans, and maybe some plants, that indulge in mock sexual behaviour, or play sex, or pretend sex. Children do that. Puppies do that. But real sex, the only kind of sex that we should call sex, is always behaviour that, in principle and by natural design, has a reproductive potential and capacity, no matter how that intent or consequence may be avoided, postponed, or foiled. To use the word for anything else is to obscure the underlying reality. Hence the debate.

Accordingly, we ought to begin by agreeing that homosexuals by definition cannot "have sex," any more than an individual can "have sex" with himself, or herself, or a bull can "have sex" with another bull. It's impossible. Homosexuals can have lots of other things, like self-administered or mutual *sensual* pleasure. No problem. But don't call it *sex*, when it can be only pretend sex.

What's this got to do with age-of-consent laws? All past societies yet to imbibe the egalitarian solvent recognized at once that, in the interests of self-preservation, the laws of society ought to encourage reproductive behaviour between consenting adults of an appropriate age, and discourage unfruitful or non-reproductive behaviour. The law, in this respect — at least until we began to confuse sex with what is merely sensual — has always been a teacher, nudging citizens in the most desirable direction and blocking intentionally dead-end, sexually sterile behaviour. In short, one reason for differential age-of-consent laws for homosexuals was to make the distinction between sexual and non-sexual behaviour. In other words — oh, let's just say it — they were set up to discourage sexually sterile relationships, or homosexuality.

So perhaps we should stop playing the puerile psychological game of pretending that we are not pretending. If we really want to encourage and protect sexually sterile behaviour in the young by lowering age-of-consent laws for homosexuals, let's have the honesty to say that this is why we are doing it.

Perhaps it is also time to recall that all good policies and laws are intended to make morally or socially useful discriminations between human actions and classes of citizens. If they don't, they have no force and effect. They are either feel-good legal or motherhood statements (like including "the supremacy of God" and the "rule of law" in our Charter of Rights and Freedoms), or general money handouts (like cutting the GST for all). But a true policy or a specific law acts otherwise. It is intended by the specifically stated force and effect of its discriminatory powers to move society in one direction, rather than another.

So it is no argument against a law or a policy to say it discriminates, when that is its very purpose and vindication.

AIDS and Mortality Rates

Basic facts about HIV and AIDS come as a surprise to a lot of people. As they should. Because it turns out that in terms of actual mortality rates, when compared with many other diseases, such as breast cancer and prostate cancer, AIDS in Canada is *a very small disease*. Almost off the radar. And yet it receives a vastly disproportionate share of funding and attention in comparison with other, far more serious diseases.

That anyone should die of any disease is upsetting. I certainly don't want to die of one, although I expect that one way or the other, many of us will. I write this as a corrective to public opinion, because I believe that the HIV and AIDS "epidemic" has been blown way out of proportion, and that knowing the truth about the situation must be the first step in understanding it.

So I sent away for the Public Health Agency of Canada's *HIV and AIDS in Canada* "surveillance" report, dated April 2005. Such reports have been produced by this agency since 1982. I also went to the Health Canada website at www.hc-sc.gc.ca, where I found, among other things, excellent information and mortality charts. I encourage you to look for yourself. Just click on the icon for "diseases and conditions" and keep drilling down. One thing you will find is that HIV and AIDS are the only conditions for which cute politicized language, such as "men who have sex with men," are used, and where there are subtle statistical efforts to cover up the facts — in this case, to hide the fact of the overwhelming disproportion of AIDS cases among male homosexuals.

Following is the comparative information (always a few years behind, because it takes time to collect mortality statistics).

PROSTATE CANCER AND MORTALITY IN 2001
There were 20,347 new cases, and 3,825 deaths.

FEMALE BREAST CANCER AND MORTALITY IN 2001
"Almost" 19,000 new cases, and "about" 5,400 deaths, each year. (The quotation marks are because these are strange terms for a statistical organization to use. Also, I have written "female" breast cancer rate in what follows, because about 1% of all breast cancer in Canada each year is found in males.)

HIV/AIDS INCIDENCE AND MORTALITY FROM 1982 TO 2003: A 21-YEAR SURVEILLANCE
Health Canada states that since 1982, when they first started keeping records, 77% of all cases have been "MSM," otherwise known as homosexual males, and they add to this the five percent of IDU or intravenous drug users who are also homosexual, for a total figure of 82%.

You have to add them yourself. Here are the deaths attributed to HIV infection (table 215, p. 64 of the report), from 1987 when the first AIDS deaths were reported, to 2002: Males, 13,503; Females, 1,205. Among these were 93 children.

OVERVIEW FOR 2006

Disease	Expected New Cases	Expected Deaths
Prostate Cancer	20,000+	3,800+
Breast Cancer	19,000+	5,400+
AIDS (projections)	200+	60

CONCLUSION AND COMPARISON OF MORTALITY RATES

If you multiply the fairly consistent prostate and breast cancer rates in Canada — which are increasing as the population ages — by the same range of 16 years as is used to tally AIDS, you get:

- *Prostate Cancer Death* (3,825/year) 1987–2002 = **61,200** total, with a climbing rate
- *Breast Cancer Death* (5,400/year) 1987–2002 = **86,400** total, with a climbing rate
- *AIDS Death* (919/year) 1987–2002 = **14,708**, with a rapidly declining rate

Note that deaths from AIDS peaked in 1995 at 1,764, and by 2002 were at 405.

Of these three diseases, AIDS is the only one communicated directly by human behaviour — overwhelmingly by "MSM" behaviour. The North American variety of AIDS is the only disease that it would seem possible to stop almost entirely by stopping the behaviours associated with it.

Readers may draw their own conclusions.

Brain Sex

In what the *National Post*'s editors called "the most controversial episode of his tenure," Harvard president Lawrence Summers has been ousted by an angry mob engaged in a kind of academic swarming behaviour unbecoming to any institution supposedly dedicated to the pursuit of truth. Summers made the politically incorrect mistake of musing that there may be "innate differences" between men and women that could explain why so few women excel at the highest levels of the maths and sciences.

In my work in progress, *The Book of Absolutes*, I have a chapter on "Biological Universals." Below are a few items from a small section of the chapter dealing with human sex differences. They are drawn from easily available sources, about facts so well known that they are uncontroversial to most scientists, despite the strenuous efforts of critics to find evidence to the contrary. Universities used to be filled with genuine scholars who wanted to know the objective truth, however unpalatable to them. Today, alas, they are overrun with ideologically stupefied academics and obsequious students who refuse to accept truths that they happen to dislike.

HORMONES RULE

The release of gender-specific hormones begins to influence human personality and behaviour even before birth. All babies begin development as females, but the male testes produce testosterone, which is the telltale hormone that fundamentally alters a baby's physical development, including the brain.

Male and Female Differences in the Womb
A great number of studies show that male and female babies behave differently even in the womb (movement, heart rate, etc.), and within moments after birth (giving priority attention to different objects, sounds, and tactile sensations).

Girls Are Sensitive to Baby's Cry
Baby girls — but not baby boys — distinguish a baby's cry from other general sounds.

Boys Prefer Objects
Although baby boys get more affection and physical contact from their mothers than girls, they nevertheless prefer objects to people.

Gendered Senses
Girls are more sensitive to sounds, smells, tastes, touch, voice, and musical nuances than boys. A girl's sense of smell is anywhere from 200 to 1,000 times better than a boy's; touch is twice as sensitive; and hearing two to four times better than a boy's.

Play Differences
Girls are less rule-bound, boys more so. Boys need rules to know if they are winning or not. Their pre-adolescent play is mostly such rank-related play.

Aggression
From birth, boys are more aggressive, competitive, and self-assertive than girls (perhaps the most common finding, world-wide, even by feminist researchers). When one-year-old babies

are separated from their mothers and toys by a barrier, the girls tend to stay in the middle of the area, and cry for help, while the boys more often cluster at the ends of the barriers, apparently trying to find a way out.

BRAIN METABOLISM

At the University of Pennsylvania School of Medicine, a combination of PET scans and high resolution MRI technology, used to study brain metabolism, showed differences, in seventeen different brain areas, between male and female brains at rest.

MALES AND VIOLENCE

At puberty, men are more prone to physical violence (most crime is by males between the ages of fifteen and twenty-five), while women are more prone to emotional volatility. About eighty-five percent of all crimes are committed by males, and there are specific, universal sex differences in the styles, types of victim, and post-crime behaviours of male and female perpetrators of violent crimes. From one-half to four-fifths of all female crime, hospital admissions, and suicides occur just prior to or during menstruation.

SPATIAL SKILLS

Boys are better than girls in a variety of spatial skills, such as mentally rotating a drawing of an object (called "imaginal rotation"), including 3-D rotation. This skill is cross-cultural, and is practically universal in males. The spatial-skill sex difference becomes quite marked after puberty, and is even observed in animals. In normal young men and women, spatial ability is directly related to testosterone levels.

LOCATING OBJECTS

Women are superior to men at certain tasks requiring memory for the location of objects. This is seen dramatically during self-location in space: women tend to do poorly at map-reading compared with men, and locate their position by memory of objects and landmarks ("turn left at the coffee shop"). Men, in contrast, tend to think in terms of compass directions ("turn north when you get to the corner"). Removing landmarks handicaps women, while changing dimensions handicaps men.

ABSTRACT REASONING

Men tend to do better at tests of abstract mathematical reasoning and *problem solving*, while women tend to be better at tests of mathematical *calculation*. This difference increases with age. Although males and females tend to get the same math scores in school, men tend to outscore women consistently on math aptitude tests. Such sex differences in math ability appear to a greater or lesser degree in all countries, and in all ethnic groups within countries.

TARGETING

From an early age, boys outdo girls by a wide margin in targeting tasks (throwing an object at a target accurately), and this difference is not due to experience or differences in strength or size. This is one of the most obvious sex differences in physical ability, and it is found in all human societies.

INTELLIGENCE DIFFERENCES

Intelligence differences between men and women are believed to be minimal, but this is because testers arrange to cancel out the obvious, repeated, and world-wide superiorities of each gender. That is, tests are arranged so that the higher verbal scores of women cancel out the higher math and spatial scores of men. But the differences in each realm, after taking overlap into account, are consistent and universal. One indicator of this difference in verbal and spatial ability is that the best female chess players in the world rank around two-thousandth among the best men, and could not gain entry to the men's world championship. Chess matches are normally segregated by sex for this reason. But world-championship Scrabble matches, and contests such as Mastermind, are not segregated by sex because there is no detectable difference with regard to those skills.

VERBAL RECALL
Women are consistently better than men at word recall, and indeed in almost all verbal tests or situations.

ENGINEERING SEX DIFFERENCES
Transplants of hypothalamic tissue (in animals) from male to female brains cause recipient females to behave in male ways.

BRAIN SIZE
The biggest difference between men and women, with respect to their brains, is size: men's brains are ten to fifteen percent larger and heavier than those of women. Men have about four billion more cortical neurons than women, and there are many structural features of the human brain that appear to be sexually differentiated.

WOMEN AND EQUALITY

There is an old French saying to this effect: "*Try to shoo Nature out the door, and she will return on all fours.*"

Caitlin Flanagan's new book, *To Hell with All That: Fearing and Loathing Our Inner Housewife,* is already making the distinct sound of determined little paws creeping back in the door. The author is an educated and financially successful woman who dares to speak out in support of so-called stay-at-home mothers.

The French saying is interesting because it is a biological metaphor of human nature as an animal, and not as a mechanical, or theoretical, entity. Point being that human nature, the biological reality of which we are all an expression, has a mind of its own, and one that, despite the efforts of social engineers to re-jig our species, will always take its rightful place. Human nature will always take over.

In Greek myth, Procrustes, the wicked son of Poseidon, had the word *Isotes* (which means "equality") carved on his sword belt. He was your typical simple-minded egalitarian (they are all simple-minded), who was so convinced that the world's problems arise from inequality that he wanted to eliminate all human differences. He was convinced that he could fix this problem all by himself and so bring justice to the world. So his solution was to subdue or drug all the travellers who came to his home for rest and drink, and then either stretch their bodies, or cut a precise length off their legs, to make them fit his bed.

This is a bizarre but telling story, so typical of the most insightful Greek myths, because it makes the immediate connection between the yearning for justice-as-equality and the inevitable outcome of extreme egalitarian regimes, which is always force, violence, and blood. The ancient Greeks knew that the ideological demand for pure equality is insatiable, like a religious conviction, and that believers will use any force, and unhesitatingly kill people who stand in their way, to make an unequal world look equal. The ancient myth foretold modern totalitarianism.

Fortunately, our social welfare states are weak versions of this psychological urge. However, they have done plenty of policy stretching, and cutting, and denying of their own, in an attempt to shoo human nature out the door. We might say that modern radical feminism has been our version of the myth. Social welfare states always embark on massive tax-funded levelling programs, the indirect objective of which is to eliminate or weaken all social institutions that are deemed to produce inequality. And the traditional family is the first and most obvious target for levelling, because some families are rich, some poor, some smart, some stupid, etc.

Plato asserted this remedy in his *Republic*, in which he advocated the destruction of marriage and proposed state child-rearing from birth in order to create a society in which "no child should know his parent, nor parent his child." Marx and Engels simply reproduced this unnatural idea in an anti-capitalist form in the nineteenth century, advocating the end of the family altogether. By the 1960s, all Western democracies were subjected to radical feminist blather about how the traditional family was only a nest for the production of patriarchy, female domestic slavery, and gender discrimination (and, yes, overeating, cellulite, and chronic depression).

Since then, untold millions of tax dollars have been

collected and spent on "status of women" projects everywhere, and most of these projects have been aimed at equalizing, if not denying altogether, the natural effects of gender. The expressed ideal when this began was to enforce absolute equality between women and men in all aspects of life. Get women out of the home and into the workforce; hire them for traditional male jobs; get their kids into daycare; give men pregnancy leave, too; train women to fight in battle; use affirmative action (reverse discrimination) to achieve equality wherever possible; change textbooks to brainwash boys and girls to believe that they are the same in all ways; give millions of dollars to pro-feminist groups, but none to traditional pro-family groups.

But the cat came back. The news is that women are finally fed up with denying their own natures. Very few women (or men) have ever seen a corner office. Killing and military violence are not something women are good at, or like. Women are "opting out of the work force" in droves. The truth is slowly sinking in that women and their families have been dupes of a kind of welfare-state tax hunger masquerading as a call for gender equality and justice.

But most such couples cannot net enough income to make a difference, after daycare and all extra costs associated with a two-income home. And yes, the tears of their children follow them to work. I know — I have seen them come back to work for me after child-bearing, and tearfully announce that they just can't bear working any longer — they want to go home.

I am enough of a libertarian to say that it is none of the state's business (and none of my business) if a husband and wife both want to join the work force, live as capitalists or communists, put all their kids in non-parental care all day, whatever. That is their choice. And there are probably a small number of families whose children would be worse off if their mothers stayed home with them. But I am trying to make an altogether different point.

Namely, that for the state to plunder the people's hard-earned income, and to intentionally lie and deceive an entire population — to stretch and cut human nature in the name of a ridiculous myth about gender equality — is a scandal.

The state could as well have promoted the natural family as the first and best choice for rearing children, and the wonderful natural differences and complementarity of the genders as a cause for national celebration. The state could have accepted the truth of human natural differences, and also the ancient moral truth that men and women are incomplete beings in themselves, with each needing the complement of the other to be complete.

At any rate, I have often ventured the prediction that the Western democracies in their deadly embrace of egalitarian ideology are *as a direct consequence* not reproducing sufficiently to replace themselves. When we see the Great Die Off coming — due to hit in the next couple of decades — these same states will hear nature's four feet loud and clear, and will roll over. We will witness a massive reversal of political ideology as all population-starved states, panicking mightily, begin rewarding, "bonusing," and, yes, favouring the traditional family, calling on all citizens to reproduce.

MOURNING MARRIAGE

Civilization is like a spider's web: delicate in the making, difficult to sustain, easy to destroy. It does not arise naturally, but is always the result of human will. But if the will becomes weak, if we drift, then the direction is always downward. Thus do all concerned citizens have a moral duty to oppose anything that undermines the common good of civilization.

Edmund Burke got it right when he said, "All that is necessary for the triumph of evil is that good men do nothing." He did not say, as we might suppose, that good men have to do bad things for evil to be victorious, but that they just do nothing. That is the reason for the downward direction of a civilization that drifts.

Battered though it has been by easy divorce and common-law laxities, traditional marriage — the only human institution the sole aim of which is to ensure that a loving mother and father are in as many homes as possible — has been the best thing for the vast majority of the kids on this planet since time began. Marriage, and the family that is its natural consequence, are institutions that have preceded — in existence, legitimacy, and prestige — all rulers, all courts, and all states.

But in substituting the term "union of two persons" for "union of a man and a woman," Canada has removed the natural biological and procreative foundation from marriage, leaving behind an eviscerated and merely legal definition — bereft of biology, bereft of what is humanly natural, bereft of custom, and bereft of any primordial concern for children. In doing so, our political leaders and courts — in sharp contrast to our neighbours to the south, where to date some twenty-eight states have passed laws outlawing gay marriage — have once again taken the easy way out by declining to protest and end one of the most foolhardy social experiments the world has ever seen.

Same-Sex "Marriage" Is Not a Right

To add shame to the sham, Stéphane Dion, the new leader of the Liberal party, tried to stir us into a fit of moral indignation by insisting that same-sex marriage is "a fundamental right" under Canada's Charter of Rights and Freedoms. But that is a distortion of the truth by an otherwise decent-seeming man. All things connected with homosexuality were roundly discussed and deliberately excluded from Canada's Charter by its framers prior to 1982. But it didn't take long for judges (who are responsible to no one) simply to decide (against the express wishes of the Canadian people, who have never given majority approval to gay marriage) that homosexuality and same-sex marriage are practices that they wanted to include under the "equality" provisions of section 15 of the Charter, where none of this is mentioned. And Dion knows this. He also knows that there is no existing human rights treaty within Canada that recognizes any such rights. Indeed, the 1948 Universal Declaration of Human Rights specifically names the family as the "natural and fundamental group unit of society," as does the European Convention of Rights, in which marriage is specifically defined as the union of a man and a woman. The German Basic Law of 1949 also gives pre-eminent right to the family, and preference in law to the raising of children by their own biological parents.

In this spirit, France has just recently repudiated gay marriage entirely, on the grounds that children thrive best with the love and support of their own parents, and should never have same-sex parenting thrust upon them, as a matter of state policy, merely to satisfy the homosexual desires of adults. The French have insisted that *wherever possible, the primordial natural right of children to know and be raised by their own biological parents must trump all adult rights.*

SAME-SEX PERSONS CANNOT "UNITE" IN "CONJUGALITY"

To avoid an anticipated public abuse of the state of marriage and a rush for merely financial and legal benefits by "any two persons," courts have ruled that these new unions must be "conjugal." Well, "conjugal" comes from the root word "to join," and any two persons can *say* that they have a conjugal union. But leaving aside the question that ought to embarrass this nation as to whether or not two penises or two vaginas can ever be "joined in union"; and leaving aside also the fact, which is so obvious to any biologist, that only human beings of opposite genders can have a "sexual" relation in any strict sense of that word; we are now in a position to ask a merely administrative question. And that question is this:

In order to qualify for Canada's considerable legal and economic marital benefits, *must* two persons have sexual relations (or mock sexual relations, in the case of homosexuals) to be considered married?

If the answer is no, then what kind of "union" is "a union of any two persons"? And if the answer is yes, then how can a state be responsible for knowing that any two persons are actually living "conjugally"? Will we now have conjugality police to ensure that "married" couples qualify? Not likely.

So then, practically speaking, why does conjugality matter? After all, there are many older heterosexual couples who no longer "have sex," as that depressingly utilitarian saying goes. Point being, if we cannot prove or disprove conjugality, how then can it be the state's test-condition to receive the benefits accruing to marriage? And if it is not a good test, then, other than the traditional requirement of heterosexuality as a presumptive condition for marriage and its benefits, what is?

WE SHOULD NOT PROMOTE WHAT IS UNNATURAL AS DESIRABLE

If this matter pertained only to individuals, I would say, who cares? Acting within the law, we ought to be able to live with whomsoever we wish, and be left alone. But this in turn means that the state — its courts and tribunals — should not be using the law to intimidate or force me, my children, my friends, or my society to agree that what other people do to excite themselves with those of their own sex is normal, or natural, if we sincerely believe otherwise. If someone chooses to "marry" a partner with whom he or she will by definition and design be barred from true sexual union, and barren forever of children, I should not be pressured or obliged to agree that this is a good idea for those persons, or for my country.

For I do not. I accept that some individuals may prefer such a life, and may think that it is good for them. But no amount of logic or argument can convince a reasonable person that it is good for society as a whole, for the common good, or for the continuation of civilization. I may think homosexuality is weird, sad, unnatural, a sexual neurosis, a disorder of the soul, whatever. But I still say — tenuously, and with much circumspection — live and let live.

Well, Bill, I am told, there have always been some childless heterosexual couples. What's the difference? Of course, there are some by choice, some by age, and some who live with the deep sadness of infertility. But a society that has intentionally privileged human partnerships that are barren by definition and thus made them a legitimate and normative model for the young, with a social status and with benefits equal to those enjoyed by unions that conform to society's difficult procreative model, is a society that has entered on a perilous course.

I say "difficult," because raising fine, honest, well-mannered, civil human beings is perhaps the most selfless daily challenge that most of us will ever undertake. It requires extraordinary emotional, personal, and financial dedication and sacrifice. And that is why it is only these unions, with the customs, laws, and practices that surround them, that ought to enjoy the venerable status in human society that has until now been reserved only for true marriage (or its common-law equivalent, as distinct from the mock homosexual marriages that we are being forced by law to accept).

We have long ago accepted the fact that some people cannot or do not wish to row the lifeboat in which we are all passengers by contributing children who, as we age and weaken, will grow up and row in their turn. We let them go along for the ride, so to speak. But it is perilous to the common voyage of our life to encourage such behaviour.

THE ARGUMENTS FOR SAME-SEX BEHAVIOUR OR MARRIAGE ARE WEAK

I have tried to find a defence of homosexual behaviour and of same-sex marriage that speaks to the common good. But there just isn't one — no reasonable biological, social, evolutionary, or health defence of homosexual behaviour or same-sex marriage.

Biologically, it is obviously a dead end.

Socially, and in the sense that our moral behaviour may be judged according to how it legitimizes our actions for others, it is also a dead end, for we should not be setting up homosexuality, or homosexual marriage, as an ideal for others.

Nor can we use the genetic or the evolutionary argument, to the effect that homosexuality provides some "survival value" for the human species, for the simple reason that homosexuals do not reproduce with each other. Indeed, any "gay gene" argument works against its proponents, for a gay gene would lead to the extinction of gayness in a generation or two. (And spare us the "helper at the nest" argument — the idea that although they do not have their own children, gays help with the child rearing, and therefore have a sort of species survival value. This is a sweet, but ridiculous, argument. And the only reason some male birds, for example, hang around to help the pair from which they have been rejected by the winning male, is in the hope of taking over next time around.)

Perhaps most dire of all is the health question. If AIDS is any indicator, homo-sex remains one of the most life-threatening practices imaginable. (Ottawa consistently tells us that over eighty percent of all AIDS deaths in Canada since the mid-1970s have been of gay males.)

Culturally? Homosexuality has been discouraged by all civilizations in history, apart from a few abnormal cliques or periods — one of which we are presently living through.

And of course, anyone who reflects frankly on what it is that homosexuals actually do with each other for their sensual (again, these cannot, by definition, be sexual) pleasures will conclude it is profoundly unnatural, just as any farmer who buys two bulls to service his herd of cows and wakes up to find them mounting each other would conclude there is something deeply wrong with them.

THE ARGUMENTS AGAINST GAY MARRIAGE ARE STRONG

These can be summed up in a paragraph or two. All human beings are born of a mother and begotten by a father, and the law and the state have always protected marriage — the mother-father-child relation — because this is the only natural means of creating human life and continuing civilization. Of high importance is the argument that marriage has always been a child-centred, and not an adult-centred, institution (until now, in Canada), and no one — no judge, no politician, and no state — has ever before claimed the right to redefine marriage so as to intentionally impose a fatherless or motherless home on a child, as a matter of state policy.

For until now, marriage has always rested on four conditions, like a four-legged chair, and compliance with all these conditions has been the condition for marital benefits. These have to do with number, gender, age, and incest. We have always said that you may marry only one person at a time, who must be someone of the opposite sex, someone above a certain age, and someone who is not a close blood relative.

But the recent official removal of the opposite-gender condition has badly weakened this stable social structure. For if it now takes only two persons to make a marriage, then why not a man and a twelve-year-old girl (breaking the age condition)? Or a brother and sister (breaking the close-relation condition)? Or what about three friends who want to marry just to cut their expenses (breaking the number condition)?

I know: marriage was already weakened by no-fault divorce and common-law relationships. But that is no excuse for smashing it entirely. We just knocked one leg off the chair, and there are already legal attempts to knock off the other three. Indeed, in the middle of my writing this piece, the Ontario Court of Appeal decided that a child may have three parents! Leave aside the argument that courts often have to appoint guardians or legal "parents," and that a child may need more than two protectors in some anomalous situations, for all that is quite different from setting up multiple parenthood as a desirable social precedent merely to accommodate homosexuals — which was the motive this time around.

This decision opened the door to legalized polygamy, and soon our Charter will be used specifically for this purpose, and then to defend such things as "intergenerational sex" (a fancy term for pedophilia). And then we will see Charter rights to "marry" a sibling, and so on. Just wait. In 1990, people thought that gay marriage was a ludicrous idea (let alone a right), and those who warned against it, such as this writer, were mocked as fear-mongers.

IF A POLICY IS "EQUAL," IT CANNOT BE A POLICY

One of the most common, but definitely among the weakest, arguments in support of gay marriage is the call for "equality." A moment's reflection will tell us that all genuine policies are intended to discriminate in a positive way in favour of some human arrangements, and not others. That is what makes a policy a policy, which is to say a program intentionally designed and targeted to achieve a specific social or economic result by *encouraging* some human behaviours and *discouraging* (vigorously discriminating against) others. However, if the test of a policy is that it must be "equal" for all, then it disqualifies itself as a policy, for it has thereby lost the very thing essential to its particular goal or purpose: the targeted discrimination or preference for certain human actions that made it a policy in the first place.

In short, if we eliminate the qualifications that made a policy effective, we convert it into a hand-out for all, which automatically loses its capacity to steer citizens one way rather than another.

Some examples of how ordinary policy distinctions discriminate beneficially for the common good are the welfare system, public awards, veteran rights, and elite athlete benefits. I am not necessarily supporting these programs. I am just arguing that if we give welfare benefits to everyone without the qualification of having a very low income, they immediately lose their policy purpose as welfare rights. And if we give all Canadians the Order of Canada, it loses its purpose of conferring public honour. And if we give veterans' benefits (let alone the Victoria Cross!) to all citizens, just to make them "equal" to veterans, the benefits lose their purpose of honouring and supporting those who have served their country as soldiers. If we give stipends to all athletes, ordinary and elite, those stipends lose their purpose of … well, encouraging those who can actually win. The same logic applies to everyday privileges like special parking spaces for handicapped people and expectant mothers — you have to qualify for them.

Just so in the case of marriage. It has always been the intent of state policy on marriage to encourage and privilege only unions that meet the four conditions or prohibitions concerning age, gender, number, and incest, and *to value them higher than any other type of human partnership.* Why? Simply because the state knows that if, with the various benefits available, you encourage enough men and women to unite sexually, you will inevitably get a lot of babies. And everyone knows that this will not be so if you reward girls for partnering with girls, or boys with boys.

At this point, people usually say, "Bill, there are only a few thousand gay marriages. What's the harm?" The response is that you can ruin the value of the Victoria Cross by presenting it with full public support to cowards, just as you can ruin the prestige of the Order of Canada by presenting it to Canadians of zero achievement. In short, to remove the qualifications for a privilege is to remove the privilege.

LOVE IS NO ARGUMENT FOR STATE BENEFITS
The state has — and ought to have — no business whatsoever involving itself as protector-adjudicator-benefactor of the private love lives of citizens for any reason, except for heterosexual marriages. Why? Because of the fact that heterosexual marriages and the children we expect and hope they will produce — about ninety-five percent of them do so — are vital for the well-being

of human society and so must be honoured and favoured above all other love arrangements, because they are the only ones with procreative potential.

At this point, homosexuals are outraged, as the fashionable expression goes, and start to protest that they love each other, too, and therefore are being deprived of an equal right. But I say, so you love someone? So what? Love is an adequate reason for demanding attention from your partner, or even from friends and relatives if they are interested in your love. But it is not a compelling ground for demanding attention from the state, or from complete strangers (citizens and taxpayers), or for insisting that equal public respect or privileges or benefits be paid to support your love. For its own sake, love can be wonderful, as we all know. But it is a private matter, and all alone, for itself, even the most wonderful private love does not justify receiving public attention, when by definition there is no hope of public benefit.

And why should it? Love is the easy part, the fun part. But child-rearing — the creation of productive and competent citizens — is very, very tough.

And that is why the only justification for extending legal protection or economic benefits, *even to heterosexual unions*, is the simple reason that society and the state have a high and justifiable expectation of getting something crucially important in return: a greater number of well-raised citizens. Without the reasonable expectation of this return on investment, so to speak, which follows with great regularity from the simple *form* of heterosexual marriage, no two people who love each other, regardless of their genders, should receive favours or protections extracted by law from anyone else.

To put it bluntly: the only kind of law-abiding private love that should be of any public concern whatsoever is the love that occurs between two people who choose to unite under the four conditions mentioned above.

And I hasten to add that in addition to diminishing the value of the institution of marriage, we are also busily undoing a distinction that our civilization has been at pains to teach us for a couple of thousand years, between good love and bad love. For it is clear that human beings are capable of loving almost anything whatsoever, good or bad (just as they may hate almost anything). In order for them to love the good instead of the bad, however, the former must be publicly recognized and encouraged by all, in morality and in law, and the latter must be discouraged. Traditionally, we discourage things like self-love in the narcissistic sense; and a crass love of money; and sexual love of children; and a love of doing hundreds of other bad things. Psychiatric manuals carry descriptions of many kinds of bad love, usually with the suffix *philia* (Greek for love), such as "necrophilia."

Until very recently, homosexual love was considered a form of bad love (and still is, by many psychiatrists, and by many citizens gutsy enough to say so), because it rests on two errors: the wrong love object, and the wrong organ, or orifice. And that plain truth cannot be changed by any number of judges or "equality" clauses.

I mention these things to explain that "love" is a rather loaded term, and though it is our deepest emotion, it cannot reasonably be used to justify getting something just because we happen to feel it. Needless to say, in this context, the suggestion that a feeling of love qualifies us to lay a claim to other people's tax dollars, in the form of social or economic benefits, is especially weak.

We Must Honour Even the Form of Natural Marriage

Okay, Bill. But what about infertile couples, or old people who marry but can no longer have children? Why should they have such rights?

First of all, because they have met all four of the qualifying conditions for marriage, with respect to number, gender, age, and incest. *That is sufficient in itself.* But I would add that they also deserve them simply because in choosing the traditional form of marital partnership, they continue to honour and perpetuate the only form of human union that (again) can be a sexual union (that has procreative potential), and thus the only kind that is absolutely essential to the preservation and continuation of civilization. Any other kind of relationship may be interesting, cute, compassionate, whatever. But from the point of view of the state, it is unimportant. It is nobody's business, and therefore ought to be of no public concern.

To repeat, citizens, simply in choosing a natural sexual union over any other form, publicly honour and acknowledge the high public value that is the foundation of this act, and in so doing, they teach this value. That is why traditional marriage, in practice and in its very *form,* must be given a respect higher than that given to any other human partnership or friendship. A society that voluntarily generalizes, demystifies, desacralizes, or simply demotes this special form of human union by offering the same privileges to "any two persons" can expect to see this once vital institution further dishonoured and mocked as trivial.

THE ROLE OF THE STATE IN MARRIAGE DEMOLITION

Citizens must beware the insidious reputation of the modern state in relation to the special role, influence, and survival of the natural family. Empires, principalities, and states, however defined, have always had one thing in common: a natural antipathy to any other human organization or association within their jurisdiction that competes with the state for the loyalty of citizens. Principal among such associations have been religion and the family, the two great social entities — the first spiritual, the second biological — to which people have always given a private allegiance more powerful than their public feeling for country or rulers.

This sort of tension was visible in ancient Rome, where the law of the family and the law of mighty Rome itself were often in conflict, the state usually giving way. Indeed, in many European nations, even today, no monarch or ruler, no matter how absolute the power, has ever had the unfettered or capricious right to enter a private home without permission of the family. But the most insidious incursions of state power into family relations and property rights have been felt since the advent of the mighty tax-harvesting social welfare states of modern times, many of which have declared an open or covert war against the private family, seeing it as a cradle of social privilege and inequality. Accordingly, they have specifically sought to weaken the natural biological bonds of marriage as the family's foundation.

Marx and Engels based much of their disastrous communist social program on a deep distrust of the private family. That was socialism with machine guns. But the softer social welfare states that arose in the twentieth century — of which Sweden and Canada are the most ideologically fervent examples — have at their foundation the very same animus against the family. Indeed, this animus exists against all biologically based distinctions, privileges, or differences between citizens that might pose a threat to the only claim of such states to a quasi-moral authority: the guarantee of citizen equality in all things.

Aware as they are that the family has a deep and powerful grip on its members for life, such states take the softer, less visible approach. They weaken the grip of the family and its privileges, not by eliminating the latter, but rather by dissolving their unique value and prestige by removing all qualifications for receiving them — that is, by showering them without discrimination on everyone alike. Just so, a deeply biologically rooted institution such as marriage can be gradually transformed into yet another vehicle for political equalization. For this, citizens — those who have not seen what is really at work — bow down and give thanks to the state

However, it seems to me that states that abandon all things spiritual and biological as the natural basis of civilization eventually find their official ideology reduced to a demoralizing and depressing concern for the mere material success and equality of all citizens. They are destined to founder through endlessly dispiriting wars over "rights." But equality, taken this far, always acts as a social and moral solvent, dissolving all formerly useful social and moral distinctions and privileges. At such a point, the old idea of justice, as embodied in what is natural and biological — with all the essential and necessary distinctions, glorious human differences, and essential social privileges this implies — will always lose in a war against the new idea of justice as simply making everyone administratively equal, by giving all, without distinction, the same privileges and benefits (for which the only qualification will now be simple citizenship — and often not even that).

In short, a fully developed egalitarian ideology must, by its own internal logic, oppose any and all natural human differences and distinctions that may threaten its only remaining, and very narrow, claim to provide justice as equality for all. I say narrow, because even the ancient Greeks, for example, did not fall for the simplistic idea that equality means justice. They did argue that one soldier must be treated like any other; and one general like another. But they never believed that a soldier and a general, a man and a boy, a boy and a girl, a fool and a wise man, or a hero and a coward, ought to be treated the same or valued or honoured in the same way.

The key difference between modern America and Canada on issues such as gay marriage — the reason three-quarters of

American states have banned it, but we as a nation embrace it — is that America has not abandoned to the same degree as Canada its traditional belief that justice must be rooted in a spiritual and natural reality. Since the Trudeau era, Canada has wholly surrendered itself to the crassly materialistic and egalitarian mentality of the welfare state, where all public debate is reduced to a kind of internal civil war over equality and rights; it is only very rarely (and with embarrassment) a debate over the good, the natural, the morally obligatory, and the true.

Needless to say, one of the last barriers to this frankly socialistic program — as any class on radical feminism will attest — has been the traditional definition of marriage as the union of a man and a woman, with all its historical privileges and protections (of late said to be patriarchal, or the origin of class hatreds). In this exact sense, we must realize that a "right" to homosexual "marriage" is not really aimed at elevating the status of homosexuality as much as it is aimed at dissolving the deep historical sense of privilege and status of true marriage, and the heterosexuality that has always been one of its four conditions.

Well, civilizations rise, and then they fall. One of the reasons they fall is that they blind themselves, first morally and then intellectually, to the natural sources of their own founding energy and success. They gradually substitute for this a myriad of laws and policies intended to extend the reach of the state into every corner of private life by eliminating all natural differences between citizens and their customs and valued institutions that might constitute a threat to the official ideology of justice as equality. We have asked for it, and we are getting it. There is hardly a better, more effective way to efface the primordial public value of marriage than to remove the words "a man and a woman" wherever they occur on the hundreds of thousands of computers and legal documents of the state, and there substitute the words "any two persons."

RESTORING THE PRO-FAMILY STATE

We see hints of it every day now. I mean, of the feeble struggle to restore the pro-family state. In recent articles we read: "UK urged to step in to save marriage" (*National Post*, March 3). The marriage rate in the UK apparently dropped by ten percent in 2005 (the most recent year for which numbers are complete), resulting in "the lowest marriage rates since they were first calculated in 1862." In fact, this trend is repeated throughout most of Europe. One brave English soul actually spoke up to say that "the government needs to abandon its pretence that all family forms are of equal value to society." He probably got sent to the Tower of London for that.

Of course, it doesn't matter how many people marry in the proper traditional sense of that word; it only matters how many children they have, because the great underlying crisis looming throughout the Western world is the gradual depopulation trend that began about twenty-five years ago. Another article, "Canadians support income split" (*National Post*, February 27), tells us that seventy-seven percent of Canadians support the idea of income-splitting that would allow "couples" to "reduce the taxes they pay by averaging out their income." There is no definition yet of the word "couples," and I will offer my own tough notions on that below. I mean, if you want to grow your country in a time of rampant individualism, with egalitarian hogswill as your public philosophy, with rabid feminism infecting otherwise healthy minds, and a marauding tax-hungry state that is always searching for more control and regulation to justify its own existence, you had better be prepared to bring in tough and *very discriminatory* tax policies. I will get to some of those at the end of this piece.

But first, the background on how we got into this pickle in the first place.

About a hundred years ago, all the Western democracies took a page from the communistic writings of Karl Marx and instituted "progressive" tax regimes under which portions of money earned through labour would be forcibly extracted "from each according to his ability," and transferred "to each according to his need." There was considerable protest at the time on the grounds of inequity. For what could justify taking twenty percent of one man's income, but fifty percent of another's? Such a regime would rob the hardest working, most productive, and most successful; would institutionalize envy; and would create an enormous class of citizens beholden to the state and its handouts.

"Equality" once meant we were all considered equal before the law. A rich man and a poor man could live as they wish, and climb or fall in life by their own hand, but each would be punished the same way for the same crime, and so on. This was a stirring standard of Western freedom for quite a while. But it was soon argued that freedom is not enough, because the rich keep climbing and the poor keep falling. None of this has ever been true, and our own government's annual report on the quintiles (fifths) of income earned have always looked about the same, despite a century of extensive policies to alter them.

At any rate, in order to bring about a world of homogeneous incomes, our once-free societies began changing the ideal of "equality" to the ideal of "equalization," and were not shy about using the powers of the state to do this. Hence little by little we began to hear more and more about so-called substantive equality — a term used for the idea that everyone ought to have equal substance in life, such as material things, food, homes, money, education, and so on.

To bring such a condition about, our freshly minted egalitarians now had to engage in unequal tax practices, just as Marx had advocated. What an irony! The equality of citizens would now be achieved by the radical inequality of citizen tax treatment.

We have now had more than a century of this civilized form of communism, or legal plunder. It is accompanied, on the part of taxpaying individuals and corporations, by a myriad of loopholes and strategies for avoiding taxation. It is further accompanied, on the part of vote-seeking political parties, by ever more schemes, as a French tax-collector put it so long ago, for "extracting the maximum number of feathers from the goose with the minimum amount of squealing."

Accompanying this morally unjustifiable but by now quite settled procedure is the corresponding tendency of all modern welfare states to "atomize" their own societies. I am convinced that over the long term, perfect social equality of the kind intended by such total states is impossible to achieve without first attacking and dissolving the freely chosen preferential forms of social life that give rise naturally to (what are now defined as) "inequities." To continue the metaphor, atomization suggests the splitting apart of a whole range of social molecules into their individual parts — that is, the breaking-down of voluntarily formed social groups (social molecules) into a collection of autonomous, independent individuals (atoms).

However, if there is a key distinction to be made here between the state and society, it is the fundamental fact that society (the sum total of all freely formed social molecules) is voluntarily constituted and has no power other than the usual forms of persuasion or dissuasion that spring from religion, morality, parental reward or censure, and so on. The state, on the other hand, is the sole entity with a monopoly on power, and in this it must be carefully distinguished from society. Your father or your priest may shame you or praise you into right behaviour. But the state can force you into it.

These two very different forms of suasion — one moral, the other legal and political — have always been in conflict. And I think it is true to say that the more total the aims of the state, the stronger its official jealousy of any competitive form of suasion. Hence, much of the effort of the state, whether ancient (such as the Roman Empire) or modern (our territorial-ethnic states), to gain more effective control of citizens has been devoted to the usurpation of the traditional moral powers of society's various groupings by breaking these constituent molecules into atoms. This is achieved by dissolving or weakening the influence of social groups over their own members, directly, or indirectly, by funding competitive government services meant to replace the same things offered privately (for example, tax-funded daycare, and tax-funded and controlled medical care); by delegitimizing such freely formed groups, services, and customs (by calling them "discriminatory," "chauvinist," "sexist," "homophobic," or the like); by burdensome or double taxation (you may send your kids to a private religious school, but you must pay taxes for public schooling anyway), and by many other means.

The underlying reasons why this process has occurred are not hard to see. The first is wealth. At the turn of the twentieth century, there were, by any measure, only about a half dozen truly wealthy nations. But by mid-century, there were more than thirty such nations, and today there are over sixty. One of the inevitable consequences of more wealth is more tax harvesting, hence the invention by governments of more vote-seeking programs, intended to grow the influence of government itself. Much of it, as mentioned above, is by substituting government services for those that individuals and social groups — such as the family — used to perform for themselves (and often, with a proud independence and a defiance of state intrusions).

Riding alongside this development, like a frenzied harridan whipping her horse, has been the modern radical feminist movement. Most of us approve of better treatment of men and women alike, where reasonable and possible, and according to the needs of each very different sex. European feminists largely think this way, and they call it "difference feminism." They don't want women treated the same as men. *They want to be treated differently from men, and better as women.*

But the dominant North American variety of feminism got stuck in the rut of radical equality. And Europeans consider us pretty stupid for having taken this gender-denial route to equality. For through a whole variety of ridiculous affirmative action and "equity policies," we have actually tried to eliminate all biological, social, and economic distinctions between men and women. At the extreme, we have even argued that gender is not something biological and natural, but something that is "socially constructed."

Suffice it to say that this philosophy — one quietly embraced and promoted by a whole string of Canadian governments, liberal as well as conservative, since the late 1960s — has fed traditional society into the equality-grinder of the state by militating against the traditional family. You know, where the man is expected to earn a decent family wage and the woman is expected to raise the kids at home.

If you want to see this program instituted with a vengeance outside communist countries, look first to Sweden, where it began in the 1940s. Canada, which used Sweden as a model, started this same program after World War II, but soon raced past its Nordic soul mate. Canada is now viewed by leftist radicals the world over as a model "autonomist" nation, where the biological basis of society has been all but neutralized or eradicated in public policy, and each taxpayer is considered an individual "economic unit" (and taxpayer) rather than part of a social or family unit, as in the past. What are some of the clues?

Canada used to allow husbands and wives to split incomes before taxation, but this was one of the first pro-family tax policies to be eliminated in Canada, as in Sweden, by the end of the 1960s. (The present Conservative government in Canada is trying to reinstate this sensible policy.) Even when socialized medicine began in the 1970s, each family was issued a family health card. But now we all have individual health cards.

In fact, all the tax schemes and policies of the past few decades are engines of atomization: national day-care plans to encourage the removal of children from families and have government workers care for them instead; unfairly burdening strong single-earner (that is, traditional) families with higher taxes; offering state welfare to all wayward youths who demand it, whether or not they come from wealthy families (another attempt to break this family tie); offering state-funded abortions to all comers without requirement of parental consent for girls over fourteen, even permitting teachers to arrange abortions for students without advising parents; removing the idea of contract from marriage and introducing divorce on a no-fault basis; and, finally, introducing the cockamamie idea of gay marriage and the whole ideological paraphernalia for shaming the population into accepting this profoundly unnatural idea on the ridiculous grounds, again, of ... equality.

Get used to it.

The loser in this program of atomization is traditional society and the myriad bonds of belonging that people will always generate if left alone. The winner is Big Government.

The current government is clever enough to introduce its income-splitting policy on the grounds of equality, too — but this time by asking why two married couples should be treated differently in the tax code just because both spouses of one couple work outside the home, but only one spouse of the other couple does so. Of course, what they are doing is pushing for a return to a family-based tax system, and a retreat from the current atomizing system of taxing us all as mere individuals. Clearly, the former strongly promotes family formation and the home-rearing of children, and the latter just as strongly discourages this — indeed, it discourages couples from having children in the first place. So I say, bravo!

Some years ago, when touring Canada with my book *The War Against the Family*, I urged exactly this kind of family income-splitting — and a few other devices to encourage family formation and procreation, to boot. I still believe that if we really wanted to populate our own country with more of our own children (rather than relying on immigration for replacement) and get ourselves above the fertility rate of 2.1 children per woman, which we need just to maintain our current level (rather than the scary nation-depleting rate of 1.65 or thereabouts, where we have been for almost two decades), we should take vigorous steps in taxation and public policy. For the timid, some of these may seem aggressive and, as such people are wont to say, "discriminatory."

But that is precisely the point. To repeat: all true public policy is intentionally discriminatory in a very positive way. It is meant to achieve a specified public purpose by application to some particular target group, and not to other groups (for to do otherwise would defeat the policy).

So if we want to push back the state, restore a strong civil society, bolster procreation and the family, and turn back the Great Die Off that is looming over the coming decades, we will need all of these ideas, or something like them. I am not a taxation expert, and I know that to make any of these ideas work would require a labyrinth of (hopefully better) laws and rejigged regulations. But the intent is clear, and where there is a will, there is a way. To the objection that these are radical ideas, I answer that they are only as radical as the ideas that have already demolished the pro-society and pro-family (and anti-statist) reality with which we began.

If you want to know what a family-friendly state's policies might look like (depending on the level of population panic), read on. (Here, LMH means "legally married heterosexual.")

1. Allow splitting of incomes for LMH couples only (a pretty strong incentive for the home-rearing of children; for scaredy-cat common-law couples to get off the pot and commit themselves to a real marriage; and to discourage homosexual unions. The French government currently permits income-splitting between all family members for precisely this purpose. A friend of mine, supporting a wife and five children on $100,000 per year, moved to France three years ago, where he now pays zero income tax because his income is divided as if earned by seven.)

2. Increase dependent-child tax credits progressively, by the number of children, payable until they reach eighteen.

3. Introduce, in addition to the aforementioned tax credits, a generous and progressively larger one-time maternity cash and tax-free bonus for each child.

4. Allow mortgage-interest deductibility for LMH couples until the last child at home reaches eighteen.

5. Index incomes of LMH couples to counter inflation and tax "bracket-creep."

6. Allow higher RRSP contributions for LMH couples.

7. Allow a generous tax credit for "same-home" care of elders, by any family member.

8. Disallow welfare for children of the wealthy. (This would help drive them back to their own families for support first, rather than into the arms of anonymous taxpayers. Mostly it would force misbehaving kids to grow up fast if they want to eat.)

9. Create business-loans insurance for LMH small family enterprises.

10. Eliminate no-fault divorce on the grounds that no-fault means no responsibility and also removes the basis of the marital contract (a true contract requires the consent of both parties to enter into or to break the contract, and breaches should entail fault and a penalty).

11. Make divorce a lot tougher for families with children — require, say, a five-year cool-off period when the youngest child is under fifteen.

12. Encourage LMH families to adopt Canadian children, with generous tax credits given for each adopted child.

13. Define the traditional family as "a married mother and father living together with their dependent children." All other forms are less committed, and ought to be less favoured in law, policy, and taxation.

14. Rigorously enforce child and spousal payments from errant fathers (or mothers).

15. Consider mothers and fathers each legally and financially responsible for their children, beginning from conception.

16. We should restrict the use of the Charter of Rights and Freedoms to the protection of citizens against government force and infringement. End its use by citizens against each other and especially against society as a whole (which would end such things as invented Charter arguments against traditional marriage and any other such hallowed traditions).

IV

Politics and Law

Six Types of Freedom

Like many people, I have a reflex affection for the word "freedom." Nevertheless, I pause when asked to explain what it means. Most people answer, "It means doing what you want." This common response speaks for an age — our own — that sees self-expression and personal satisfaction as the key to authenticity. But throughout history various cultures and civilizations have had vastly different concepts of freedom, and even within our own tradition the meaning has never ceased to change.

For example, the Greek sense of freedom differed from the Roman; the earliest Christian ideal of freedom differed radically from its later one; freedom in the Renaissance meant release from the supposed darkness of religion and a return to the enlightened classical past; by the eighteenth century freedom meant living by the light of pure "reason"; and then, in the Romantic period, from about 1780 to 1830, people revolted against the idea of cold and heartless reason and sought "true freedom" in feeling and original self-expression.

In the middle of the nineteenth century, classical liberals (as distinct from their modern brethren who are pro-statist) began extending this idea into political life, demanding freedom from all unwarranted authority — especially that of the state.

And finally, our most recent ideal of freedom is a rather paradoxical one: we want a combination of radical individual rights, but also a vast social security net to be provided by the welfare state. This uniquely modern combination we may think of as a kind of *libertarian socialism*.

At any rate, as the concept is so multi-faceted, a single definition of freedom is almost impossible to find. So I have been wondering if a better approach might be to construct a working classification of the different *kinds* of freedom. There are at least six of these, as explained below. But first, there is an all-important distinction to be made between *freedom* and *liberty*, as these two words are often used interchangeably.

I propose that the word "liberty" should be used to refer to freedom in its physical context, and not to other kinds of freedom. A man in jail, for example, has almost zero liberty but retains all his freedom in the sense that he has not lost the ability to choose among myriad options, attitudes, and values. He can sleep, count the miles while pacing the floor, or write poetry. He can also decide to lie to the warden to protect a fellow criminal, or tell the truth.

Most people, it seems, use their freedom to restrict their liberty in all sorts of ways. For example, selling oneself into slavery for a few years used to be common in the ancient world. Sometimes whole towns sold themselves as slaves to a neighbouring city in exchange for military protection. And there have always been people who have chosen to become hermits or monks, voluntarily restricting their liberty in the hope of finding spiritual freedom. Less dramatically, most of modern life for everyone is spent freely getting tangled up in all sorts of ways that reduce liberty. We use mortgages, bank loans, contracts, leases, business deals, and family and personal promises and obligations as free choices to restrict our liberty. Indeed, a bit of reflection will reveal that most human beings most of the time build a lock-step kind of life for themselves ... and then complain that they would like to be freer.

With this distinction hopefully cleared up, I now want to describe the six different kinds of freedom that come to mind.

INTERNAL FREEDOM

The first and most basic type of freedom is embodied by the chap in jail. He has all his internal freedom, but no liberty. All normal human beings are born and remain free in the most important sense that they are forever and at every conscious moment freely choosing beings, and every life is a delicate tapestry of millions of such personal choices, for better or worse. We cannot escape this kind of freedom even if we try, for we must then freely choose between means of escape, and so on.

From this perspective we are condemned to be free, for even choosing not to choose is a choice. Internal freedom is of the greatest personal intimacy and secretiveness, indeed it is the hidden core of our being and unknowable by others. It distinguishes human beings from the animal kingdom, and from each other, and is the basis on which we are able to become moral — or a-moral, or immoral — beings. That is why some people call this moral freedom.

But this kind of freedom is not in itself moral. Rather, it is the unique capacity we have to become moral or immoral according to how we use our freedom.

SELF-FREEDOM

Most of the world's freedom talk, at least as found in the great religions and philosophical movements, has had to do with freedom from ourselves, in the sense of learning how to escape the ever-present danger of enslavement by our own passions and ignorance.

For the ancients, self-freedom had to do with the practice of self-control, restraint, and balance to achieve the admired master-slave relationship of soul over body that they were certain was essential for the good life.

In modern times, however, this ideal has largely been turned upside down with the expression of strong feelings, of the "true self," elevated to the superior position. The goal of this kind of freedom is therefore often expressed as the need "to find my self" (although no one ever seems to ask how we would know whether the self seeking, or the self sought, is the true self). At any rate, this inversion of the traditional relation of mind over feeling, according to many, has produced what our forbears would have called a disorder of the soul. But whatever may be the outcome, few moderns ever escape a lifelong dialogue with themselves on this kind of freedom.

EXTERNAL FREEDOM (SOMETIMES CALLED "FREEDOM FROM")

This refers to the normal and common freedoms expected in daily life, in most countries, throughout history. It is sometimes described as *freedom from*, because it implies immunity from undue interference by authority, especially by government. It is also sometimes called "negative freedom," meaning freedom to do anything *not forbidden* by the laws (in contrast to a totalitarian system that says you may only do what is *permitted* by the laws). Many in the Western tradition consider this, in combination with political freedom, explained next, to be the most important kind of freedom.

POLITICAL FREEDOM (SOMETIMES CALLED "FREEDOM TO")

Try to imagine a world in which you are ruled by a tyrant who lets you do what you want on Monday, but not on Tuesday, and so on, unpredictably. You would likely conclude that whatever your external freedoms may be, they are too unpredictable to be of any use.

What we might call "political freedom" has to do with establishing certain predictable and permanent *rights* of action (whether we use them or not) and *limits* to government power that help to guarantee the practice of those rights. The most common political freedoms are the right to speak freely, to associate with people of your choice, to own property, to worship, to leave and re-enter your country, to be tried by a jury of your peers, to vote in elections (if you live in a democracy), and so on.

When these rights exist, we can say we have freedom to do these things (though to speak truthfully, we are only free to do them if they are permitted). They comprise the normal rights associated with a free society (which may or may not be a democratic one). For example, ancient Athens had all these things but was not democratic in our modern sense of the word (up to a third of the citizens of Athens were slaves). England had all these rights fully two centuries before she became democratic. The former Soviet Union, on the other hand, promised all these things to citizens on paper, but did not allow them in practice, because the only sense of freedom expected there was collective freedom.

COLLECTIVE, OR HIGHER FREEDOM (SOMETIMES CALLED "FREEDOM FOR")

Many commentators on freedom take the view that external freedom and political freedom are just formal concepts that mean nothing to the poor and disadvantaged. Indeed, in this view, they often amount to a recipe for a chaotic liberal society, an uncivil nightmare of clashing wills and unconnected citizens chasing bucks to see who can die with the most toys. What is really needed, they argue, is a "higher freedom" based on a collective will to achieve the common good.

This is sometimes labelled "positive freedom," or "freedom for," because it is based on an ideology of collective unity that prescribes distinct social and moral values and objectives for all. For example, often under this ideal of freedom the state alone is allowed to control the production and supply of all basic citizen needs, thus giving them freedom-from-want.

Believers in collective freedom say the idea of protecting citizens from their own government is not logical if the government is the embodiment of their will in the first place. Needless to say, this type of freedom, in the name of which we have seen disastrous totalitarian experiments in our time, is the deadly enemy of the sort of political freedom found under liberal constitutionalism.

SPIRITUAL FREEDOM

In its purest form, this type of freedom comes from striving for a complete identification with God (or God's will, or all creation, for example) to arrive at a condition of soul that transcends the confusion and disharmony of the self and the material world.

There are many types here, but at the extreme some seekers after this kind of spiritual freedom take one of two opposing routes. They engage in a kind of libertinism of the flesh on the ground that the body is of no importance whatsoever and so may be used, abused, and enjoyed until it is spent (pot-smoking hippie mystics come to mind). Or they take the ascetic route and deny the flesh altogether on the ground that worldly needs, pleasures, and longings prevent achievement of complete spiritual freedom (I think of my Buddhist neighbour here). For this type, strict control of, if not denial of, the allurements of the body leads to complete freedom of the spirit.

So there you have it. This effort in distinguishing the types of freedom will be repaid if the next time someone asks you what freedom means, you may in turn ask: "To what type are you referring?"

In Defence of Capital Punishment

It would be nice if we had a capital punishment debate worthy of a vibrant people, instead of the national excuse for one that lies drugged and dormant beneath a political blanket, awakened occasionally when some public figure pulls back the sheets, only to prompt the reflex reaction, *quick, cover it up!*

Meanwhile, we groan to learn that about eleven hundred convicted murderers are out on day parole in Canada at any one time. We know, with high certainty, that some will murder again. Those responsible for their release will pass the buck. A Toronto man recently left his favourite restaurant trembling when he saw a new waiter approach, none other than the man who had murdered his daughter nineteen years earlier.

If ever there was an issue to sharply outline the clash between the democratic masses and their academic and media elites, it is capital punishment. The people want it. The elites do not. Generally, the people take the moral view of crime and punishment and the elites the therapeutic view. Elites say the only motive for killing as punishment is revenge. They generally believe that crime arises from its conditions: the perpetrator can be no more responsible for his crime than for an abscessed tooth. They say therapy — not some punishment as barbaric as the crime — is required, because the criminal is sick.

The British writer C.S. Lewis wrote a famous essay in 1949 criticizing this therapeutic, or humanitarian, view of justice, contrasting it neatly with the retributive view. The therapeutic view of justice sounds nice because it appears to be mercy-based. But the hidden danger is that it dehumanizes us all by conceiving of man as a determined object with no will of his own (otherwise he could have said no to the crime) and therefore no moral responsibility. It is thus a view that, once adopted, automatically diminishes all of society by shunting justice to a secondary position.

Lewis much preferred the second view that retribution — restoring the balance of justice — was fairer both to the community and to the criminal. He summarized his critique in a telling statement about "just deserts" (what is deserved), as follows: "The Humanitarian theory removes from punishment the concept of Desert. But the concept of Desert is the only connecting link between punishment and justice."

And for making decisions about just deserts, he felt his barber was as qualified as any therapist, who may be well qualified in theories of the subconscious, but no more so than the barber in the matter of moral justice — which is necessarily a community affair. The people are the jury.

For a century now, the therapeutic view has increasingly been used to separate punishment from justice, as if man were perfectible mechanically. But in the face of ever more barbaric crimes, it is surely time to ask a simple question, namely: *Can a society maintain civility if it prefers individual mercy to collective justice?*

And never mind the merely utilitarian, and by now useless, criteria for assessing the viability of punishment: Does it incapacitate? Does it deter? Obviously, we do not incapacitate a vicious murderer by paroling him. Nor by releasing him after a euphemistic "life" sentence of fifteen, or even the maximum twenty-five, years. Neither can deterrence ever be properly measured when all punishment is delayed, lenient, and invisible to the public.

The highest and best argument for capital punishment for premeditated murder is society's need for and right to equity — for *moral restoration*. It is a right higher than any possible right of a murderer to enjoy the gift of life after the death of his victim. Justice should oversee mercy, not the reverse.

And importantly, the balancing satisfaction of retributive justice, even as it purges individuals of any lingering desire to kill, sends the ultimate message that killing for justice is a right of society, not of individuals; that such moral accounting must always be transferred to the larger society, where it belongs. This balancing of the books is required not because it is effective. Or a deterrent. Or because it may reform others. But simply because it is just.

Neither is it true that all deaths are equal. Any death is regrettable. But a salving, or expiatory, death does not treat a criminal "as something less than human," as *The Globe and Mail*'s Andrew Coyne once wrote. Quite the contrary. It is the highest and best way for a murderer to die. It is a retributive death, a form of repayment that gives meaning back to society, as well as to the criminal's soiled life, in fact lifting him out of the animal condition to which he has consigned himself. We must consider that this, too, may be called an act of mercy. That "He paid the price, fair and square," may not be such a bad epitaph.

The mistaken modern liberal notion that the issue of capital punishment concerns primarily the rights of the individual criminal is deeply defective. And it most certainly creates a climate for heinous crime by implying that society has no transcendent claim to equity; in fact has a lesser claim against the murderer than he made against his victim.

False mercy can never produce a cohesive people, or a truly merciful one, because it makes us all accomplices in undermining justice.

An Elected Senate? Be Careful!

I have been corresponding with a colleague over the idea of an "elected Senate," which is something high on Prime Minister Stephen Harper's list. Here is the essence of the issue, for me, at least.

"Parliament" in our system consists of two Houses, not one, as we often think. It is composed of an elected House of Commons and an appointed Senate. This is our heritage from the British system of political and moral checks and balances, which for centuries has been considered one of the most prudent systems ever invented. That system was deeply influenced by the Roman ideal of balancing the human and political realities of emotion and reason, and not by the Greek ideal of radical democracy, of the unchecked Will of the majority. Some of the thinking can be found worked out in a treatise on government from the second century B.C. by the historian Polybius, who, in his attempt to explain the success of the Romans, wrote *The Rise of the Roman Empire*. In Book VI of that treatise, we find the classic formula for the "mixed constitution." Put briefly, and in my own words, the system he describes is "humane" in that it is based on the model of a human being waging an internal war between democratic interests — warring emotions within, struggling for victory — with the cool head of reason making the best choice after the heat of emotion has passed.

Putting these two concepts together in a single parliament was meant to provide us with something *better* than mere democratic impulsivity: the warring factions of "the People." In other words, the whole purpose of having an upper house is that it is intentionally *not* controlled by the same partisan emotional politicking that stirs the people below: the commoners. And there is no doubt the metaphor of the human being does suggest that raw emotions are more animal, more common, grip us with passion and deceive us, and therefore are lower in value than calm deliberation and reason. That is why, under this theory, the Senate most definitely ought *not* to be an elected body. The democratic voice of the people should still be heard, of course, but it should be a voice filtered, checked, and disciplined by cooler heads above the fray.

In an interesting twist of trans-Atlantic political history, it was the Frenchman Charles de Montesquieu who, after studying the English system, added to the whole mixture the idea of not only balancing and checking powers, but also of *separating* them so that none of them — the legislative, executive, or judicial bodies — could become dictatorial and control the others. In the formation of what is now the world's oldest "democracy" (you can see why that word is a bit of a misnomer), in the years leading up to the writing of the American Constitution in 1787, the American founding fathers often had recourse to thoughts of Rome and Montesquieu. Today, Washington, D.C. is full of somewhat pompous faux-Roman, rather than Greek, architecture, because the very history of political experience, and especially of political disasters, pointed to the balanced Roman model rather than the impulsive Greek democratic one. All this was and still is an implicit *institutional recognition* that unchecked Will, whether in persons or parliaments, is always a recipe for trouble.

So where are we now? It seems to me that in the scenario I have painted here, the cry from the people to elect a Senate must be considered something akin to a child's cry for attention and control, because that is simply what he wants — right now! Carrying the metaphor further, try to imagine a teenager protesting to a parent that it is time he got his way without any correction. In the same fashion, the cry for an elected Senate is an expression of the radical democrat's outrage at the idea of having his almighty Will checked, filtered, or just plain cooled off, by anyone else.

Now let's suppose that this impetuous democratic thrust is successful in Canada. What could the result be? One result, I fear, is what might be called "a conflict of legitimacy," under which, if both houses are elected, each can make a justifiable case that it is thereby the only true (the truest?) representative of the people's will. For if we do end up voting for both, which one could we say was, after all, indeed the truest? For make no mistake, in a struggle over a piece of legislation crucial to this nation's future, we could very well end up with just such a conflict of legitimacy, expressed or implied. That is the very structure of such an arrangement in which both houses claim to represent the people directly.

Seems to me that the original and rather noble ideal of an appointed senate came from an earlier time when it was commonly believed possible to find and place statesmen instead of politicians in upper houses. A politician has been defined as someone who is worried about the next election, and a statesman as someone who is worried about the next generation. That is quite a difference. Despite all the evidence that the statesman ideal is already a dead duck in our moribund Senate, I am reluctant to surrender it. I think we should fight to maintain it, and should teach it to our kids at home and in school as a desirable ideal. For of one thing we can be certain: once the concept of competing political parties invades discussion in the Senate, that ideal will be deader than dead.

Despotism and the French Revolution

Alexis de Tocqueville's brilliant study of the French Revolution and the *ancien régime* (old system), published in 1856, laid out a thesis about the French Revolution and the modern democratic ethos that was so original — perhaps "shocking" is a better word — that it was pretty much ignored for more than a century. No one could believe it. No one did. And so by the early twentieth century, French historians were like clones, presenting an orthodox Marxist-socialist interpretation of the Revolution as a historical shift from feudalism to capitalism, marked by class struggles involving various liaisons and conflicts between workers, bourgeois elites, land-owning nobility, and so on. Almost without exception, all these historians saw the revolution as a glorious anti-monarchical undertaking in the name of the people and human liberty that — oops! — got derailed by the Terror of 1792–1794, during which time there was an organized violence of the new democratic state against full French citizens at a level of cruelty and bloodiness not equaled again until the time of Hitler and Stalin.

While they glorified the Revolution as an impassioned, noble struggle for liberty, these historians conveniently disowned the Terror and the guillotine, describing it as "a break" from the Revolution's true historical course.

By the 1980s, however, all such interpretations had simply collapsed, because a new kind of conservative history was emerging (about the time of the Bicentennial celebration of the

Revolution in 1989 — when the Berlin Wall also collapsed). These new historians were far less ideological and much more scrupulous about studying actual historical documents rather than imposing a personal, party, or materialistic ideology on past events. It turns out that they were rediscovering Tocqueville's thesis.

His main point had been that the "democratic" French Revolution was not, as so many had concluded, a breaking away from an oppressive aristocratic or monarchical past. It was, rather, *a continuation of the ancien régime, and the dictatorship of Napoleon was its natural conclusion.* In effect, Napoleon was a new monarch of the people, newly crowned by the democratic ethos, so to speak. The kernel of this reasoning was that in making the centralized democratic state so powerful, and by investing individual citizens with a concept of their own egalitarian nobility, gleaned from the radical theories of Rousseau — in terms of which *each citizen saw himself as embodying the unchecked Will of the entire nation* — the revolutionaries had actually continued the prior despotism under a new name. The old solitary sovereign was gone, but now each citizen was a sovereign (and a despot) in miniature.

In the name of this new collective sovereignty (which Rousseau had called *la volonté générale*), the French people imposed an oppressive tutelary power over themselves, greater than any monarch in history had ever exercised. (It is remarkable that Canada's Prime Minister Pierre Elliott Trudeau had a life-long affection for Rousseau's idea of the General Will, which, although he misunderstood it somewhat, he used often in public speeches and in his writings. He considered Canada's Charter of Rights and Freedoms a kind of French code law, Rousseauist in spirit.)

The man who led the new "revisionist" school of history was François Furet, and his major work, *Interpreting the French*

Revolution, published in 1978, pretty much incorporated Tocqueville's thesis. By the time of France's Bicentennial, Furet had become the new dean of French historians and was highly respected worldwide. This was somewhat of an embarrassment for the French at the time, who were reflexively firing off millions of dollars worth of firecrackers, even though Furet and his now very powerful revisionist school had demonstrated from clear historical evidence that the French Revolution was *not* the old story about glorious human freedom and national liberation that had been forcibly rammed down every student's throat for two hundred years.

In short, this school argued that the Revolution did not "break," as had been claimed by so many historians eager to glorify egalitarian democracy, while repudiating the bloodshed to which it led. Furet and others were able to show that the Revolution was not spurred by economics or concrete materialistic class warfare. It was, in fact, highly ideological and abstract in nature: it was the extreme democratic ideas of radicals like Jean-Jacques Rousseau (especially in his tract *The Social Contract*) "that had become the heart and soul of the French Revolution."

In other words, from its first day, the trajectory of the Revolution pointed toward the eventual total control of a state using radical democratic ideology to rule in a despotic manner. It was a continuous event, and its underlying egalitarianism led inevitably, like a train on iron rails, to the guillotine, and to the pointless slaughter of almost a quarter of a million French citizens.

For those interested, there are some good books to read.

First is *The French Revolution: Recent Debates and New Controversies* (New York: Routledge, 1998), by Gary Kates. It has a superb introduction on the essential changes in recent writing about the Revolution, and contains a collection of short essays, including one by François Furet himself, to illustrate the trend. One essay in particular, "Constitution," by the American Keith Baker, running only fifteen pages, describes the whole sorry business in careful detail.

Also very valuable is Baker's book *Inventing the French Revolution* (Cambridge University Press, 1990), which dissects the course of the Revolution, as if looking through a spy-glass at the French debates of the time about freedom and equality. It shows step by step how such debates can lead otherwise sensible people to justify murder in the name of liberty.

For those who want a less scholarly but still intensely interesting, approach, look for *Paris in the Terror* by Sanley Loomis (New York: Lippincott, 1964). It has three main sections, on Marat, Danton, and Robespierre, respectively, and starts with Charlotte Corday's murder of Marat in his bathtub. It grabs you like a good novel. Unfortunately, it's out-of-print now, but you can find it at www.abebooks.com.

SWEDISH AND CANADIAN SOCIALISM

The first thing to note is the coldly reasoned language of the key Swedish policy-makers. When Swedish radicals (I mean radical egalitarian socialists), as early as the pre–World War II years, decided that their population was not growing because of "modernization" — by which they meant the effects of contraception, secularization, materialism, "free love," and so on — the fear that Sweden might one day disappear started alarms ringing. The feminist scholar Alva Myrdal decided that because the old family "model" of a wage-earning father and a stay-at-home mother was not producing sufficient children, Swedes clearly needed a new model. She declared that "declining population rates should be fought with increased gender equality." This idea went dormant at the start of the war, and remained so for the next couple of decades, but by the 1960s and 1970s her double-earner family was all the rage.

What was peculiar and very clever about Myrdal's "solution" is that it reversed the normal idea that the way to get more babies is through the traditional family form. Instead, Myrdal and company seized on their looming population crisis to introduce radical pro-feminist reforms. Any nation needs to produce 2.1 children per female just to maintain the population, and more than that to grow. Produce fewer, and the country basically dies off. Sweden's Total Fertility Rate, or TFR, in the post-war years was about 1.6. — clearly a crisis for a small nation. (Canada's rate has been about 1.6 or less for more than twenty years now.)

Somehow, as American Sweden-observer Alan Carlson points out, Myrdal persuaded Swedish policy-makers and legislators that "a full equity feminist agenda [was] the answer to the fertility crisis spawned by modernity." Carlson describes her program thus: If European peoples "want to survive in the 21st Century ... they should eliminate the full-time mother and homemaker, banish the family wage concept [under which males must be paid enough to support a wife and three children], end the married-couple home as an economic institution, welcome out-of-wedlock births and non-marital co-habitation; push all women — especially actual or potential mothers — into the labour force, enforce strict gender equality in all areas of life, engineer men into childcare-givers, and embrace expensive state allowances, parental leave, and public day-care programs."

The result should be more babies.

So influential was the Swedish model that by 2004, the European Commission had proposed the "harmonization" of all European family policies on "the Swedish model," stressing a de-emphasis on marriage and a more aggressive "individualization of rights" (as distinct from the legal and economic rights and protections of family units). Under this radical model, the family home would rapidly lose importance as an economic and legal unit, to be replaced in significance by umpteen state programs and subsidies for just about everything the families formerly provided for themselves. There would be new subsidies for clothing, schooling, school food allowances, daycare, sex education, a "bachelor tax" to encourage marriage and procreation, "free" universal health care, low-interest marriage and housing loans, more public housing, free contraceptives (to encourage early and guilt-free sexual activity in the young), and also free abortion to ensure that all Swedish children were "wanted children."

The Swedish social welfare state was now encroaching with unprecedented force and influence on voluntary civil associations such as the family, and substituting its own coercive programs and services for those that family and community members normally and historically provided for each other. Major changes were required for this revolution in social policy to have its full effect.

The most important was in the area of public philosophy. Around 1969 Myrdal and company simply declared that henceforth all Swedish citizens would be considered *individual economic units*, and that in the eyes of the state "every adult is responsible for his or her own support."

This led straight to the most powerful device for dissolving the traditional marital home — the tax system. Sweden had always had a "joint" tax return. In effect, if a mother stayed at home and was not in the job market, with a husband earning a good family wage, both parties were allowed to split his income prior to taxation, and then both would be taxed at a lower combined rate than if the husband alone were taxed at the high rate rate. By ending this system, Sweden effectively introduced a form of tax punishment for the single-income-breadwinner family home.

Carlson points out that modern analysts of the Swedish situation — and we must note here that *Canada has implemented all of the Swedish policies in the past few decades* — "are nearly unanimous in viewing this shift from 'joint' to 'individual' taxation as the most sweeping social change in Sweden over the last 40 years, for it 'more or less eradicated' the traditional home."

From 1972 on, under the new social-democratic government of Olaf Palme, with Alva Myrdal as one of his cabinet ministers, all of the aforementioned policies were embedded in Swedish society with a vengeance.

Swedish policy wonks crowed about their new "andro-gynous" individual and the death of the male "provider" and the "housewife," and all this was codified in 1987. The Swedish state would now be "neutral" as to family form; the new laws would apply equally to heterosexual and homosexual couples. By 2002, gay couples were granted the right to adopt. And Swedish courts have recently recognized polygamous marriages among Muslim immigrants. It is predicted that general polygamy will be allowed by 2010.

Carlson summarizes by saying that all of this represents the victory of three historical revolutions: the victory of the Industrial Revolution, and its principles of economic centralization, specialization, and efficiency, as against the mutual interdependency of the family home and bonds; the victory of a legally imposed abstract "equality" over natural gender differences between men and women; and finally, the victory of the socialist ideal of coercive collectivism over the free, voluntary, and traditional human associations that were formerly self-sustaining, without state control or interference.

Big Brother has been here for a while. And here's food for thought: Sweden's radical policies have never even approached the stated goal. In 2005, Sweden's TFR was 1.54 children per woman.

SOCIALISM: THE ULTIMATE CONSERVATISM

Allow me to describe what I call the "political sandwich." It is a political structure composed of:

- *The state* at the top, distinguished by its monopoly on power
- *Society* in the middle, composed of the countless civil associations into some of which we are born, but into most of which we enter voluntarily (and that are distinguished not by power but by various forms of moral authority — familial, religious, corporate, etc. — from all of which we can walk away by choice)
- And the autonomous *individual* at the bottom who, conceived solely as an individual, has control over himself, but who nevertheless exists politically and involuntarily under the power of the state (in the sense that he cannot change or escape this), yet who, as an adult, binds himself voluntarily to the various forms of social and moral authority under which he lives daily

We may think of liberalism in its original, classical form as in a sense an anti-statist but not anti-social ideology that promoted first and foremost the flourishing of individuals, and saw society as a product or sum of the human actions of individuals. Such a liberalism resisted all undue power from the top, but accepted that individuals may choose to submit themselves to various forms of authority from the middle as a means to their flourishing. (This form of liberalism no longer meaningfully exists. It ran off and reconstituted itself as modern libertarianism.)

So what happened to liberalism in its classic form? Beginning at about the mid-twentieth century, it came to the conclusion that the free market forces and individual rights it had always espoused were, in fact, freezing all sorts of people into have and have-not social and economic classes. And so this liberalism rapidly morphed into our contemporary form of "social liberalism," by drawing on the full power of the state to enforce what was now a modern liberal vision of human life. Liberalism was now a pro-statist, rather than anti-statist, political philosophy. Trudeau brought about this transition almost single-handedly, and by force of personality, in Canada.

Liberalism thus surrendered its older concept of "formal" equality, under which it had expected each free individual to flourish, and substituted for it a socialist-style concept of "substantive" equality, according to which, because it deemed all of us to be inherently equal, the powers of the state must now be used to level or equalize the lives of all in material, rather than merely formal, terms.

Conservatism we may think of as a political philosophy that has existed since ancient times and that values most highly the middle of the sandwich. It values freedom, property rights, and a market economy, as did classical liberalism. However, its valuation of these things is not absolute. It is qualified by the balance of costs and the benefits provided, not only to the individual, but to society itself conceived as an organic whole, or being, with an importance prior to and greater than that of all individuals.

Conservatism sees the individual as a moral agent free to choose between good and evil, but insists that the quality of this freedom is acquired through the process of civilization.

Conservatism insists that freedom is not important in itself, for in itself it has no meaning. We need freedom, so that we may freely bind ourselves to what is good, of permanent value, to be cherished, to be conserved. In this sense, the fully developed individual — rich in manners, generosity, and respect for others; vital; and humanly productive — is created by the voluntary efforts of society, and not the other way around.

When such true conservatives have sought to restrict personal or economic freedoms, they have ostensibly done so in the name of the greater good of society. (Please leave political party conservatives out of this who, like politicians of other stripes, have often hidden behind this idea for personal gain.) Society, in this vision, has a character and being of its own, a tone, and civility, the elevation and protection of which must be of concern to all.

We may think of the socialist as a person who wants passionately to bring about a good and just society, as do the others mentioned here, but who defines this as an egalitarian condition of substantive (rather than merely formal) equality for all. That is his planted axiom, so to speak. And that is why his focus is on the top, or power level, of the sandwich, rather than on the bottom (he rejects individualism), or the middle (he sees a free civil society as a collection of privileges for the powerful few). This is also why he so dislikes inequities of income, property, and social class, and it is why the pure socialist sees private property as the fundamental evil dividing all men.

Although he knows power is coercive, the socialist is ideologically committed to using it as a means to remake and perfect political society. In this sense, the socialist and the social-liberal are almost indistinguishable, at least insofar as they each support the modern welfare state (although the doctrinaire socialist sees the welfare state as only a stop along the way to real political perfection via socialism).

Now, even though it is true that conservatives are reluctant to change, prefer time-honoured traditions, respect religion, honour the family as the centrepiece of society, and so on, it is manifestly untrue that conservatives are against all change. It is true, however, that a conservative prefers a live cat to a theory about cats, and a live farmer or tradesman to a theory about the working class, and so a living and reasonably functioning and happy society to an intellectual's Cloud-cuckoo-land social theory. For him, society is like a spider's web: intricate and delicate in the making, but easy to sweep away. So while not against change in principle — society and tradition are always slowly changing — he is against ill-advised change that proposes to destroy, in the name of some egotistical, abstract, theoretical scheme of possible perfection, what is working reasonably well now. For him, the abstract idea of what is best is always the enemy of what is actually better.

It is normal to hear that the socialist wants "progress" but the conservative does not. The latter is always accused of wanting Ozzie and Harriet, or of being "a dinosaur." But this should give us pause. For just as the Muslim jihadist wants democracy — one man, one vote, once, in order to end democracy — the true socialist wants "progress," only once (which pretty much steamrollers the meaning of "progress").

Hence, the socialist's ultimate aim is to destroy the multifarious levels, distinctions, differences, and privileges of ordinary society through progressive policies, and replace them with an egalitarian society never before seen in human history. It will be a society in which all material things are owned equally by all; private property is forbidden; all incomes are equal; no social or economic privilege is allowed to arise; the family, but for the needs of breeding, is destroyed as a socially privileged and protected entity, and all children are raised equally by the state; and all social classes will cease to exist.

And this will be brought about, not by persuasion, but by the use of power. And it will never change. It will be the most "conservative" society that has ever existed.

QUEBEC A NATION? NEVER!

Somebody pinch me. Professor Michael Ignatieff, once a contender for leadership of the Liberal party, wanted to campaign on the supposed right of Quebec and aboriginals to form their own "nations." But what is a nation? Surely it is a territory containing a people with common civic interests and laws, with a legally constituted sovereign government that defends boundaries recognized and accepted under international law? If he means a "culture," then he ought to have said so. We all have our cultures. But since 1867, Quebec has been a province of Canada, and not a nation.

So what was Ignatieff talking about? Seems to me that he proposed something that runs contrary to the will of the Canadian people, to the Senate, to Parliament, and to at least nine provincial legislatures, something that openly challenges the Constitution of Canada. Yet aside from some media reaction questioning his judgment, there was tepid public reaction — perhaps because most Canadians are understandably tired of the whole topic, and have never been given straight answers to fundamental questions. Such as:

WHO GIVES PERMISSION TO SEPARATE AND FORM A NEW NATION?

In a heated radio debate against Bernard Landry when he was a big shot with the Parti Québécois, I asked him, "Why do you think Quebec or any other province has the right to separate?"

Without hesitation, he blurted out: "Democracy. We have been a democracy for tree-undred years!" Then he cited the tiresome idea that all any separatist party needs is "a majority of fifty percent plus one vote" to recreate itself as a new nation.

His eyes glazed over when I argued that neither Canada nor any of its provinces has ever been a simple majoritarian "democracy" in the sense that he was implying. Our Parliament makes our law, not the people directly, and in fact the whole contraption is structured to prevent the very majority steamroller that he wants. I also argued that the idea of fifty percent plus one, besides not being legal, is not sensible either, for it means that if one-half of the people in a province say no, and one half say yes — in which case, both sides are legitimately opposed and balanced — *a single citizen could walk into a ballot box and decide the entire destiny of Canada.* That has always been the weakness of direct democratic methods attempted within federations.

Fortunately, Canada is a federal state, a constitutional monarchy with representative democracy, not a direct democracy. And one of the founding motives in its original design was to avoid, if not make impossible, the very sort of democratic destruction of the nation that separatists have imagined.

By contrast, the core idea of federations is that they have a tangible and legal reality that is more than the sum of its parts. As constitutional lawyer Stephen Scott of McGill once said, it would be "disastrous for constitutional negotiations to proceed on the premise that a province, if dissatisfied, can overthrow the state," for no federation could possibly survive being based on such a premise. Rather, in all federations serious national matters are decided, not by the opinion of one-half of any political party, or subordinate group, or territory, but *by the whole union acting according to the law of the Constitution.* Canada's Constitution already has a perfectly good *legal* amending procedure (in

Part V) that could be used to arrange the separation of any province *if the people as a whole wanted it.* But this section specifies that no province of Canada has the legal right to alter boundaries without the consent of the House of Commons, the Senate, and all the provincial legislatures. *Any other method would be a revolt against the government of Canada.*

WHO DECIDES WHAT MAY BE TAKEN?

In the unlikely event that a province ever won the legal right to form itself into a new nation, as above, struggles would arise over property rights. For Canada as a whole belongs to the people as a whole, regardless of where they happen to live. It is not as if by living in Ontario today, you have some legal property claim over your proportionate share of that province, and then by moving to Alberta next week, you surrender this, and now claim a new proportionate right over a piece of Alberta. Quebecers do not "own" Quebec any more than Albertans own Alberta.

Canada is not like a condo, in which each apartment (or province) is owned by some specified citizens and not by others. It's more like a building with twelve rooms (provinces and territories) that is owned-in-common by all. So a small group trying to rip a province or territory out of Canada would be like someone trying to chainsaw a room off the building without the permission of the other owners. And it happens that most of Canada's territory and property inside Quebec boundaries was originally placed under Quebec's jurisdiction to be administered *as a province of Canada,* and not as a separate nation. So Canada would probably and rightfully claim a good deal of it. The truth is that Canadians, through their government alone, have the right to decide on all terms and conditions for the break-up of their country, on debt repayment, or on land settlement, under the laws of the Constitution.

Can We Separate from Separatists?

This is the Catch-22 of all separatist arguments based on the fifty percent plus one idea, because any argument successfully used to legitimize the division of Canada can as easily be used to legitimize in turn the division of a maverick province. In Quebec, native people and anglophones would quickly seize upon separatist-style arguments either to remain there in Canadian enclaves, or to create their own new provinces. During the last so-called referendum (it was really a unilateral provincial plebiscite, not a legal national referendum), one group of anglophone Quebecers campaigned to form "Quebec West" as a new nation. Only force can stop this domino effect, once separation on such flimsy grounds is condoned. That is why you can vote your way into most federations, but not out of them.

So the truth seems to be that under the laws of Canada, there can be no unilateral referendums by provinces to decide the fate of the whole nation; no unilaterally declared "nations" formed inside the nation of Canada; and no unilateral claims by provinces to sovereign territory or property belonging to all Canadians.

How long must we endure politicians so eager to secure Quebec votes that they are willing to suppress these nation-binding truths?

Choosing Your Belonging

There are some things about which concerned citizens must speak up, and here is one of them.

In one of his campaign speeches, Liberal leadership candidate and professor Michael Ignatieff, attempting to lure Quebec voters, said, "The great achievement of Canada, and I think we're already there, is *in Canada you're free to choose your belonging.*"

By "already there," he meant that his modern liberal vision of citizenship has already been realized. For he went on to say, "You can be Quebecer first and Canadian second, or Canadian first and Quebecer second," and then added — and this is what struck me — "*in the order that suits you.*" If what we are choosing is our citizenship — the basis of our national loyalty — then Ignatieff is a spokesman for the bizarre idea that the basis of national citizenship is self-chosen.

Just look back to the last time the Canadian nation as a whole decided to confront the international peril of totalitarianism on the European continent, by defending, among other nations, Britain and the British Commonwealth — the source of our political system, our freedoms, our common law, and the dominant culture of the Canadian people. At that time this sort of "choosing your belonging" was vigorously manifested by many thousands of young male Quebecers who, though they were born here and cheerfully accepted all the rights and benefits of Canadian citizenship, chose to decline the responsibility of fighting alongside their Canadian brethren to defend those rights and benefits. What they were choosing, really, was that it was okay for us to die for them, but not for them to die for us. By the time this trial balloon for "choosing your belonging" ended, and Quebecers were conscripted, we were all Canadians, all one, and they proved to be great fighters.

But what this illustrated was that "choosing your belonging" is not a sound basis for citizenship or nationhood. For every nation must decide from the very start what it stands for, who is to qualify as a citizen, and how the nation as a whole will control and defend its territory, its national character, and its long-term ambitions. To suggest, as Ignatieff has done, that the provinces or states of which a federation is composed may compete with the unity of the federation as a whole for the primary loyalty of citizens is to argue that there is no federation worth the name. Canada may defend itself this week, but not with Quebec-Canadians, or Albertan-Canadians, or Ontarian-Canadians. Next week, however — if, say, our oil supply is threatened — Canada may defend itself with the latter group, but not with Newfoundland-Canadians, who have their own oil. It would be everyone's choice.

Now, what is the origin of this idea? It is, I believe, a desperate response to the reality that Canada as a determined and unified nation — I mean a nation determined to define itself culturally, morally, religiously, and politically — has lost its way. Canadians individually may embrace Ignatieff's idea of choosing their own belonging, but Canada as a country would thus have no national will to self-determine. We do not ask ourselves what we are or want to be.

But what is the point of maintaining a nation that has no way, that is blown hither and thither by the winds like a ship at sea with no course or destination? To put this question in perspective, let us imagine that tomorrow we will start over, forming ourselves into a new nation. We would have to choose between all available systems of government on offer, choose a dominant language for business and government, a core religious tradition, a legal system, a set of core customs and civil traditions, and the like.

I believe that if all such choices were laid before us, we would very likely choose a parliamentary system much as we now have, with English as our dominant language. We would include the ancient common-law traditions and customs we have enjoyed for so long, and we would also opt for the Christian religion as the source of our moral code and the underlying foundation of our civil, legal, and political understandings, such as the value of persons and property, *habeas corpus*, and so on. And we would likely insist that immigrants to our new country share and defend these aspects of nationhood, or seek their happiness in some other land. We would not allow them to choose "what suits them" as the basis of our national loyalty.

But what is Canada actually doing?

Another *National Post* item tells us that an expected "supertanker" of Chinese immigrants has in fact turned back because "China's interest in Canada as a place to live is on the decline." Then we are informed, without emotion or comment, that "Canada's racial face is about to change." Notice the passive sense used here. The item does not say that we as a nation, a people with control of our own destiny, have decided to change our racial face (here, for race, you can substitute national language, religion, legal system, and so on), but that some force outside Canada — a "demographic shift" — will decide this for us. We learn that the "foreign springboard" will soon launch a majority of immigrants from India instead, who will bounce into Canada, where the Indian community, "with all its domestic political resources," will "continue to widen the flow." Seems that a Ganges river is about to pour over our land.

What are Canadians to make of this demographic shift? Who has made this decision to alter the face of our nation in this way? A Ms. Wilson, speaking for Citizenship and Immigration Canada, was careful to stress that *it is not we, the people, who have willed or expressed a wish for this change.* She informs us — again without emotion or commentary — that the federal government's immigration program is "demand driven." And she adds, "We don't tweak it in any way, or impose quotas."

What this means is that the type, speed, and direction of alterations to the fundamental fabric of the Canadian nation and its people — its legal, religious, linguistic, cultural, and moral profile, and institutions as we go forward into the future — is being decided by non-Canadians. By which non-Canadians, you may ask? Holding what beliefs? Willing to defend what traditions, laws, and customs? It doesn't seem to matter. As a nation and a people, we seem content to remain undefined, undetermined, with no concern about what we become. In other words, we are being led into the future by strangers.

If that is what we want, then fine. Let's openly and proudly choose not to choose what suits us. But I don't think anyone in recent memory has asked us. At any rate, whatever it is we think we belong to now, will not likely soon be here. Whatever. As long as it suits someone.

Rae's Rambling Rhetoric

On the editorial page of the *National Post* (November 7, 2006), Liberal leadership candidate Bob Rae — formerly of the NDP, and once the premier of Ontario, for a mercifully brief period — warned us to "reject those who suggest there is a fatal flaw in the Canadian idea."

Perhaps this warning is a little self-serving, rolling as it did off Bob's own lips, along with a lot of other misleadingly glib observations. For the "fatal flaw" is Bob himself, along with all those other pretentious political puffballs with which so many political parties seem infested, who wake up every day with their strangely "Canadian idea" of "leadership" — a word that they all fancy applies to their own chosen role in Canadian life. However, his warning merits a little scrutiny.

Bob's article feels good. Like so many other politicians, he has mastered the art of saying nothing at all in carefully selected phrases of non-commitment to anything (except the nearest rhetorical escape route if questioned too closely), or of saying what is not, in fact, true, but presenting it as fact and history.

We are told that "Canada's Constitution was, in 1867, an act of the British Parliament." He then says, "it took over a hundred years before it became truly ours [in 1982], with an entrenched Charter of Rights and its own amending formula."

But this was precisely the point at which, for many Canadians, the Constitution became *untruly* ours. For, in effect, on that date it left the hands of the Canadian people and became

Trudeau's, and Bob's (along with all their benighted leftist kin). Indeed, with these remarks, sly Bob revealed the real cleavages in this country.

First, we have a population cleavage, because millions of us old enough to remember can honestly say we grew up in a different place prior to 1982. From 1867 until then, our legal and political system rested primarily on a venerable, centuries-old common-law tradition; the provinces more or less exercised their own precisely enumerated provincial powers (which have always been distinct from those of the federal power); and we had a representative democratic parliament through which our will — captured in the laws that we thought it wise to promulgate — was expressed by our representatives in the House of Commons. Once ratified, those laws became the highest law in the land. I mean the highest statute law, of course, because citizens of British-style common-law nations always held (as we did until 1982) that there are certain rights and duties of citizens to liberty, property, *habeas corpus*, religious expression, etc., that since Magna Carta in 1215 A.D. have been supreme, even over the will of Parliament, and all courts.

But Trudeau's (and Rae's) beloved Charter changed all that. No Canadian since 1982 can now truly say that the laws of the land express his or her will, or even the will of the Canadian people, simply because the Charter is now the supreme law of Canada, and only unelected judges may decide what they believe the words of the Charter to mean. So the true and fundamental meaning of that change was, and is, to hell with the will of the people. There are two practical reasons why this is true.

First, because our elected representatives simply will no longer bother to propose a *new* law (no matter how good they, or we, think it would be for the people), which they know an ideological court (like most courts these days, whether left or right) will shoot down as soon as they look at it.

And second, because all *existing* laws dragged before such courts now have their previously established meanings reconstituted, not according to what the judges honestly believe the people intended when they made those laws, or according to the force of case law over the centuries, but according to what the judges personally believe the law ought to be. In other words, since 1982, at almost every turn, the opinion of judges is being substituted for the voice of the people.

Now, I think it bizarre that prior to 1867, voices were raised in tumult over, and many lives were even lost in the clamour for, "responsible government." Canada's settlers insisted on the right to make their own laws through their elected representatives, rather than have them handed down by the British parliament and courts. We finally got bits of responsible government by the 1840s, and got it fully by 1867. But there is a good case for claiming that we surrendered it again in 1982, for at a single stroke of Trudeau's pen, we effectively removed the right — and the expectation — of the people to make the supreme law of the land, handing that right over to our own courts.

I suppose that is better than handing it over to the British courts once again. But not much. Point being, we no longer have responsible government in the sense of having the right to express our unfettered will through unfettered representatives. Say what you may, we had them unfettered for a while, but now they are fettered anew. And I would say this whether the courts were leftist or rightist, because the principle is dead wrong in and of itself, for it surrenders us to judicial oligarchy, of whatever stripe.

Like so many others who gleefully rearranged Canada in 1982, Bob is out there once again, promoting himself and his leftist views. Note how he closes: "Leadership is about building confidence through success in addressing the practical needs of Canadians. Above all, we need to address the real imperatives of our era. These include acting on climate change, building a prosperous economy, providing jobs for Canadians, maintaining an independent and thoughtful foreign policy, ensuring a competitive tax regime, reducing child poverty, supporting learning."

Please forgive my cynicism. But it is surely outdone by Bob's own. So allow me to recast his remarks by way of offering an alternative vision.

"Leadership" is about stopping the growth of meddlesome, over-regulating government at all three levels, so that the people can regain the confidence that comes from running their own lives, families, and livelihoods responsibly. It is about recognizing that no one really knows anything about the reasons for climate change. We don't even have the slightest idea whether or not it is actually changing, and if so, why? So we should keep the planet as clean as we can personally, locally, and nationally, without using supposed climate change as a cover for more taxation, more socialism, and more regulation.

As for "building an economy"? Aside from the prevention of force and fraud, and the enforcement of contracts and the law, we should get out of the way of the people when it comes to commercial affairs and entrepreneurship. And we should also stop giving businesses money that is taken from the hands of so many ordinary citizens who can ill afford to part with it. Governments cannot "build" economies. They can only create an appropriate framework for them. As for creating jobs? We know only too well that every job the government "creates" to make itself look good costs taxpayers more than the job itself ever pays back to the country. In this sense, so-called job creation is just another form of vote-buying welfare.

Most of all, we should burn as much government red tape as possible so that vital and imaginative young Canadians will think about staying in Canada to work, invent, and invest, instead of heading south after we have spent $100,000 educating them.

And foreign policy? Canada is a very small country, with what is perhaps a disproportionate political clout, because it is perceived by other countries as decent. But we need to stop congratulating ourselves on our pretended moral superiority and stop spending untold millions on useless, mostly leftist, foreign causes, because we cannot afford it, and anyway, in the long run, the countries that we assist simply have to learn to fend for themselves instead of waiting for handouts. Too often, international "aid" enfeebles other nations.

When it comes to our "tax regime," child poverty, and learning, we should take the position that the least tax is the best tax, and leave as much of the people's income in their own hands as possible, to use in steering their own lives.

Also, it is a myth that corporations pay taxes. They do, of course. But all corporate taxes are just passed on to consumers in the price of products. So in that sense, only consumers pay taxes.

True child poverty is very rare, because most parents would rather die than let their children starve or live in want. So the first and best way to deal with poverty of any kind is to strengthen the roots of the traditional family by encouraging marriage over common-law partnerships, by chasing down deadbeat dads who don't support their own wives and kids, and by tax cuts and incentives to families to look after their own elderly parents.

Finally, there is learning. Our universities are still good, and some of their departments are even great. But modern campuses have too few serious students, and too many who are there mostly for a tax-funded holiday from reality, and for partying. Everyone loves a good party. But subsidizing education for rich kids, or for the growing drug and party crowd, or as a means of vote-buying or cozying up to corporate research at the taxpayers' expense, or tolerating the Gentleman's B grading system and handing out degrees to all comers regardless of genuine performance, or giving deadbeat professors tenure? Well, we can "support learning" by taking a clean broom to the whole business.

From History to Harper to "Nation"

In asking Parliament to endorse a motion "that this house recognize that the *Québécois* form a nation within a united Canada," our Prime Minister has dictated the terms of what could be a protracted debate over sovereignty. The fact that he also hobbled his Liberal and separatist enemies and befriended the wily province (or is it "the nation"?) of Quebec at a single stroke was fascinating. But it was immaterial to the much larger question that has plagued both American and Canadian federalism from the start, namely, can there be a state within a state? Harper was careful to head off this question when he added: "Do the Québécois form a nation inside Canada? The answer is yes. Do the Québécois form an independent nation within Canada? The answer is no, and the answer will always be no."

But to understand what he is up to and the long-term stakes of his motion, we need to revisit the constitutional logic of our own history.

As it happens, the Constitution of the United States of America, thrashed out in 1787–1788, and Canada's British North America Act of 1867 were both among the boldest efforts ever undertaken to resolve the ancient problem of *imperium in imperio*, or "sovereignty within sovereignty." The challenge recognized by both nations was to find a solution, and both were certain that they had done so. But in this writer's opinion, both sets of founders, were they here today, would say that their fondest hopes and intentions for their constitutions — their respective solutions — have been betrayed.

The background for the American settlers, and by extension for Canada, was the relationship of the original American colonies to the sovereignty of Mother England. The Americans at first attempted to gain independence without severing their ties to the Crown. But their British masters insisted that *imperium in imperio* is a solecism, or a contradiction in terms, that can never work: the colonies could not be governed by England and *also* by themselves, because sovereignty is by its nature indivisible. In words that were as prophetic for the Americans as they are now for us, the loyalist Thomas Hutchinson asked, "How can there be a *subordinate* power without a power *superior* to it?" George Mason, too, insisted that "two concurrent powers cannot exist long together; *the one will destroy the other.*" And Patrick Henry declared that a mutual concurrence of powers "will carry you into endless absurdity."

The Englishman James Galloway had warned that no one had ever squared the sovereignty circle before because it cannot be squared; it is "unintelligible jargon, and horrid nonsense," simply because "the notion of two sovereign authorities in the same state is a contradiction, a monster!"

These warnings were still ringing in the air when the Americans achieved their independence in 1776, an independence made inevitable largely due to the fact that a sovereign America under a sovereign England had indeed proved a monstrous idea. So, once free of Britain, the thirteen colonies began to operate as thirteen independent democratic states.

For a decade, chaos ensued. Most of them immediately raised their own armies and navies, and some seized each other's ships. Seven of them printed their own money (including inflationary fiat money, if that suited them), fought interminably over borders, and passed tariff laws against each other. And, on several occasions, mobs of angry farmers swarmed their own legislatures, demanding that laws be passed to forgive their debts. Some of the new states even eliminated their own senates (because they wanted to remove all obstruction to their will), and in one state, the mob called even for the elimination of its own legislature: each town could rule itself!

Alexander Hamilton, one of the brightest lights among the American framers of the new Constitution, aiming to end this madness, famously complained that the thirteen independent states had become "wretched nurseries of unceasing discord."

So it was high irony indeed when the founders met in the summer of 1787 to frame a constitution for their vast territories, and found themselves making the same arguments that England had made with respect to the former colonies. For how was a single government to administer America? Were its officers expected to travel three thousand miles of wilderness to do their business? Of course not. Now they could see why Montesquieu, whose teachings at the time were so influential, had already warned that a unitary democratic government can only work in a small country.

And then there were the facts: The thirteen states were already sovereign in their own right. They would be meeting now to delegate, to surrender, powers they already had over themselves, to a new general, or central government. This meant the newly united states would need two levels of elected government — state and federal — which in turn meant there would be two sources of popular will that could erupt in conflict any time. And that is why the debates over the very shape of the new Constitution of the United States came to centre on the problem of how to tame the monster. The system the Americans eventually settled on became the background for Canada's rather different solution in 1867.

The American camps were divided into "federalists," who wanted power to be more centralized (their emphasis was on the word "united"), and "anti-federalists," who wanted more powerful local rights because they were terrified of all forms of centralizing power (their emphasis was on the word "states"). This they equated with the English tax slavery from which the colonies had just escaped; they were not going to set up the same despotism in their own house! So in the end, the states delegated a list of specified general powers to the new central government, and kept all their own local powers. The individual states also retained all "residual" powers, or the right to any unforeseeable future powers that might be required.

As a further restraint, the Constitution of these newly united nations (now to be states) rested on the novel idea of "checks and balances," of breaking sovereignty into pieces through a division, a balancing, and a sprinkling of it between competing institutions of government — the courts, the legislature, the senate, and the executive — so that none of them could amass too much power and become a tyrant over the people. Even so, a sorrowful critic of this new arrangement, in a wonderful phrase, decried the powerful new office of the President as "the fetus of monarchy."

But the abiding faith was that this new two-level sovereignty-within-sovereignty would be limited by carefully defined and restricted powers, each in its own realm. States would look after things *internal* to themselves, while the feds would look after all things general, or *external*, to the states. For the one thing feared by all — federalist and anti-federalist alike — was the idea of any government that could creep into every corner of the country, that would "wait upon the ladies in their toilett ... accompany them to the ball, the play, and the assembly ... enter the house of every gentleman, watch over his cellar, wait upon his cook, attend him to his bed-chamber, and watch him while he sleeps."

In today's lingo, the common enemy was any tax-harvesting, over-regulating government; which is to say, they all feared precisely what America and Canada have become today. Then, taxation hardly existed. Today, the average Canadian family forks over forty-six percent of income annually in total taxes, for a lifetime.

On paper, at least, the plan seemed to make sense for governing a widely dispersed people. And because the lesson of the bloody French revolutionary experiment with democracy, and also the wretched discord of the thirteen states themselves, were both still fresh in memory, the "democratic element" to be included in the Constitution would be democracy by delegation. The expression of the popular will via "representation" was invented as a way to keep the rabble from direct law-making. That is, to prevent too much democracy.

The new Americans (and later, the Canadians) wanted instead a "filtered" democracy, relying on a "natural aristocracy" of wise and elected representatives, expected to make laws for the whole people, not merely for their own local electors, and who would have senators not directly elected by the people presiding over them to further chasten the popular will. There would be no more mobs of farmers swarming legislatures and changing the laws to suit themselves.

What became of this noble experiment across the line? History has provided the sad story of America's losing battle with the monster. The first, and most dire, wake-up call was the dreadful, nation-splitting outcome of the Civil War, which although ostensibly fought over slavery, was at bottom a struggle between states' rights (among them, the right to pass local laws about slavery) and federal rights (the right of a central government to forbid state laws). Very few of the new centralizing powers invoked to win that war have since been repealed.

Then came the nation-mobilizing pressure of two world wars, with their new taxing powers. Between the wars, there was the even more centralizing reality of relief efforts, during the Great Depression.

But perhaps the *coup de grace* to states' rights was constitutional dickering, such as the fourteenth amendment, which gave the US federal government massive powers — a constitutional primacy — permitting it to disallow state laws.

More recently, there have been huge increases in the dictatorially intrusive powers of the courts, which, against the founders' intent, have now set themselves up as the sole authority on the Constitution. Prior to this change, the people (via the amendment procedures), and even the President were acknowledged as the principal interpreters of the Constitution, and not the courts.

The consequence of all this is that America has become something very close to an invasive, hyper-regulatory unitary state — a monster. The contradictions of *imperium in imperio* have been borne out there, the superior powers of Washington, Congress, and the courts having extended a net of control over all subordinated powers.

And what happened to Canada? We began with a sense of superiority and a prideful optimism that we would tame the monster better than the Yankees had done. In 1865, John A. Macdonald set the Canadian tone: "Ever since the [American] union was formed, the difficulty of what is called 'States' Rights' has existed, and this had much to do with bringing on the present unhappy war in the United States. They commenced, in fact, at the wrong end. They declared by their constitution that each state was a sovereignty in itself."

In short, Canadians wished above all to avoid the clash of sovereignties that had reduced the United States to the rubble of civil war. So of the many differences invented, perhaps the most significant would be our special way of dividing powers, not as in the republic over the border, but in a novel Confederation. The Yankee states had delegated a list of specified general powers to their general legislature, but had, the Canadians thought, mistakenly left everything else — all the things unspecified — to the local legislatures. The Canadians thought it better *to specify the limited and exclusive powers of both legislatures*. In the new Canada, there would be a list of *general* powers for the general government, and a list of *local* powers for the provinces.

Ours would be a system of *coordinate sovereignty*, with neither entity sovereign over the other *in its own realm*. It was thus that, through a pragmatic division of powers in what became the BNA Act of 1867, Canada's founders were satisfied that they had tamed the monster once and for all by restricting the sovereignty of provinces to what was "assigned exclusively" to them (their "list"), but also by permitting the general government to make laws for "peace, order, and good government" in relation to all matters *not* among those assigned exclusively to the provinces.

It was no small condition, either, that in order to prevent excessive local power received by spending beyond their means, the borrowing power of all the provinces was restricted by law to their "sole credit." Also in contrast to the American system, our federal government (rather than local governments) would look after all unspecified general matters.

Canada's monster-taming scheme worked well for almost a hundred years. By that time — 1968, the advent of the modern Liberal effort to socialize Canada — we had a total debt, after an entire century, of only some sixteen billion dollars. But as in America, the mobilizing force of *imperium in imperio* is always the lust for superior sovereignty — indeed, for *total* sovereignty. And the trend over time is always that the superior power will find ways, however devious, to slowly gobble up the subordinate ones. (It is a process that has also been at work at lower levels, where the provinces gobble up municipal powers — just ask any mayor!)

At any rate, the federal and provincial gobbling in Canada has been achieved in a variety of ways, including, of course, through direct legislation, but especially via so-called shared-cost programs in which the federal government has circumvented the wise constitutional constraints of our founders on provincial borrowing. It has done this by harvesting money through exorbitant taxation of individuals and their corporations (a corporate tax is just a pass-through tax on individual consumption), and then offering to share with the provinces the cost of many things that under our Constitution were intended to be controlled "exclusively" by the provinces (such as health care). They have offered to do this in exchange for the provinces' submission to central control in those matters. In other words, this form of central control has been gained through bald fiscal bribery, aiming at a flagrant evasion of the very constitutional prohibitions — the wisdom — intended to prevent it.

Perhaps the most disturbing expression of this impulse to control local jurisdictions and ideologically to reshape even the most venerable customs and traditions of Canada, has been via Supreme Court rulings since the creation of the 1982 Charter of Rights and Freedoms. Many of these rulings have in effect rewritten our Constitution by repealing wise common-law judgments and customs, but especially by "reading into" the abstract words of the Charter meanings that unelected judges, who represent no one, simply believe should be there. This autocratic centralizing process began gradually in Canada, but accelerated with a vengeance during the 1960s.

This was the period when Lester Pearson, with his justice minister, Pierre Trudeau, alongside him, remarked that in effect being the Prime Minister of Canada was the closest thing to being a dictator, if you wanted to be one. Later, in 1969, when asked by a reporter, "What society would you like to make Canada? Socialist or capitalist?" Prime Minister Pierre Trudeau replied, "Labour party socialist — or Cuban socialism or Chinese socialism — socialism from each according to his means." By the time he ended his time in power, Canada had two hundred billion dollars in federal debt alone, and another trillion in unfunded government liabilities (promises to pay future benefits). That two hundred billion, at the rate of interest since then, comes to the almost six hundred billion in federal debt we carry today.

Through this socialist process of taking from each according to his means, and giving to each according to his need (Karl Marx's most famous slogan), the regions of Canada were divided by fiat into giver and taker provinces. The country had also experienced one of the most massive and rapid expansions of civil service of any free nation in history. Ottawa informs us that today we have one full-time government employee for every five Canadian citizens. But if we think only of taxpayers, it comes to something more like one full-time government employee for every two or three taxpayers.

It was into this pregnant history, this top-heavy consequence of *imperium in imperio*, that Stephen Harper walked when he first entered political life as a Reform Party member in 1990. Now he is our Prime Minister. What kind of man is he? By training, he is a free-market, if not a libertarian (anti-statist), economist. By religion, he is an observant Christian, who feels in his bones the importance of individual moral agency and personal and local responsibility. He holds dear the crucially important social role of marriage and the traditional family, values the importance of self-reliance and meaningful work for all, and looks for a strict observance of law. For all these reasons and more, he believes that the best government is the least, and the more local it is, the better.

Which is to say that our new Prime Minister belongs to a venerable "anti-federalist" (in the sense of anti-statist) tradition, through and through. By instinct and where possible, he will choose "subsidiarity" as his moral and political guide: Let us solve our problems first at the lowest possible level, and then rise for help to each successive level, only when absolutely necessary or specified by the constitution. Let us fight back against big-taxing and hyper-regulatory socialism. Let us bring about a devolution of power, placing responsibility locally where it belongs, where it operates most efficiently, and where Canada's own founding fathers were certain it would stay if Canadians simply chose to abide by their own constitutional constraints.

The case shaping up here is that Mr. Harper is, like this writer, in the Canadian context *a conservative revolutionary*. He believes that nations ought to live by their own constitutional commitments, and if they want to change those commit-ments, it should be by proper constitutional means, and not by the sort of cheating legal stealth and fiscal bribery that has been used to convert Canada from a well-balanced constitutional confederation into a centralizing welfare state now carrying a total debt (including unfunded liabilities) of over three trillion dollars.

He knows this is a system that cannot sustain itself. No such system has ever succeeded beyond a few generations. They are always taken down by structural debt that they cannot escape, by the demoralization that always follows the removal of essential individual and community bonds and responsibilities, and by the politics of regional envy — the war between have and have-not regions — leading to fluctuating allegiances (Am I a Canadian? A Quebecer? An Albertan? A hyphenated-Canadian?) and hence a loss of any true national identity. Which is to say, by *imperium in imperio*.

So it must be undone. There must be a rebalancing, devolution, and restoration of assigned constitutional powers; a restoring of states' rights, so to speak. Canada must be returned to something resembling its original constitutional framework by withdrawing federal powers from all places where they have never by right or by law belonged.

Such an initiative, which I submit has just begun, will — or has the potential to — turn Canada back from its foolish reliance on a socialistic model, to something more in keeping with the vision of our founding, a Confederation. A good real-world example of this at work today, one that produces an extremely high standard of living, is Switzerland. Most of the conservative moral, fiscal, and political principles outlined here have held sway there for many centuries, and peace, productivity, and freedom are maintained in a democratic nation with twenty-one provinces (called cantons) and five distinct language groups.

And yet it is ironic in the extreme that Quebec has never followed the socialist model imposed on the Rest of Canada. And that is because Quebec has always insisted on building its own socialist model *within* Quebec. However, for socialism to work, it must always be total, and no small socialist state can survive inside a larger one. That is why Quebec has fought tooth and nail for its own constitutional provincial rights and more, and in exchange for its block voting power and four or five billion a year in transfer payments from the rest of us, it has gotten them. She has fought for the right to control her own language laws, her own pension plan, her own immigration selection, education policy, and a hundred other matters large and small.

In effect, Quebec has merely done what all the provinces ought to have been doing all along: fighting to preserve all those provincial rights "assigned exclusively" under our Constitution, and pushing back all centralizing intrusions of power wherever possible.

For entirely different reasons, this initiative is also catching on elsewhere in Canada. For the past two decades, Alberta has been flirting with the same anti-centralizing psychology, though far less successfully, because it has less with which to whore in terms of voting power. But because Alberta has always been a giver and not a taker province, many Albertans are today pushing for just such a devolution or rebalancing of sovereignty, including a restoration of provincial control over their own exclusively provincial matters, such as for the privatization of medical care, a provincial pension plan, and more.

So, in conclusion, what we have before us, under the rubric of a qualified nationhood for Quebec, is in fact the first bold step in reversing the Canadian welfare state. Harper is keenly aware that no one will now dare to deny Quebec its new "nation" status. He is also aware that Quebec will now likely support him for a majority government in the next election. And he knows that Quebec will continue to push for the powers appropriate to a nation. But he will hold them to what he said: Quebec will be considered a nation "within a united Canada."

And he will then slowly apply that condition to all other provinces that want it, because under our Constitution, provinces were intended to have provincial sovereignty over their own list, and the feds were to meant to keep their hands off that list, and to respect provincial sovereignty in a united Canada. Of course, the other provinces, not as dominated as Quebec by a single ethnic and linguistic group, will not care if they are called a "nation," but they should be labelled something just as chummy. What they will insist on is "equal" provincial rights and sovereignty.

Thus, through a long process of reversing the workings of the monster — including the reduction of taxes wherever possible, elimination of the national debt, removal of nanny-state federal tentacles from all places in which they have never by right belonged, and, of course, by removal of transfer payments — he will undertake to restore provincial constitutional rights. Harper has just commenced the deconstruction of our rusty welfare state. He aims to slay the monster and restore us to our own constitutional truth and honesty.

THE CHARTER AT TWENTY-FIVE

We have been treated of late to a variety of opinions published in various media concerning Canada's 1982 Charter of Rights and Freedoms, which is now twenty-five years old. In the opinion of this reader, however, the real story of the Charter and its damaging consequences was ignored by the press.

In my opinion, when it is told by future historians, it will go something like this: Prior to the founding of Canada under the *British North America Act of 1867*, all those in the British colonies of the New World lived under English parliamentary law, and their court proceedings were judged according to common-law precedent. Law made by parliamentarians was the highest law of the land. But even before deciding on new statutes, English parliamentarians would usually make passionate appeals to common law, because in the public mind, such precedents were considered a precious historical inheritance from what G.K. Chesterton called "the democracy of the dead." Which is to say, a priceless gift of moral and legislative wisdom from our ancestors, near and far.

In the rising democratic spirit of the times, however, these Canadians-to-be once or twice revolted against British rule to achieve what they called "responsible government." By this revolutionary slogan, they meant that they wanted those who made their laws to answer to them, the people. They were finished with colonial governors bossing them around, responsible only to the English Parliament in London or the

Privy Council some six thousand miles away, for neither entity had any obligation to answer to those over whom they ruled. And their government had gotten a little more responsible by the 1840s.

But it was only with the BNA Act of 1867 that Canada finally got fully responsible government. The new Canadians would now grow their own British-style parliamentary tradition and common-law inheritance (with the exception of Quebec, which would also use French Code law), and would at last have political masters responsible to them alone. They would finally be able to hire and fire their own lawmakers.

This hopeful regime lasted a mere 115 years, until 1982, when Prime Minister Trudeau got the Charter he wanted. Now, among the things that Trudeau had always mocked and despised were English concepts of governance, such as common law. He was very much unsettled by the idea of ten provincial legislatures all making their own sovereign laws, sometimes in conflict with each other. Of course, that right of sovereign law-making by local citizens was a mark of the glory and freedom of the English system. But to a francophone intellectual, the very idea of a nation without a unitary Napoleonic-style code hovering over it, which like a magnet would orient all political and moral iron filings, was abhorrent.

In short, Trudeau despised any system under which "the people" in Parliament (and in each provincial legislature) had the unfettered right to create statutes that were by definition "the highest law of the land." This complaint is typical of anyone raised in the Cartesian intellectual tradition, in which rational conclusions are supposed to flow from fixed axioms, and laws must follow clear and distinct principles, rather than emerge from potentially conflicting precedents. That means that laws must be shaped by a rationalized higher code, and to hell with the common-law insights of ancestors. What did they know about modern socialist theory, anyway? Nothing, of course, so forget them, was the feeling.

What Trudeau wanted, and got, was a new, abstractly worded code-law, to be imposed on the freedom of legislators in Canada's Parliament, all provincial legislatures, and courts. The meaning of all the articles of his Charter, if challenged, would then be decided by unelected judges, who were above the democratic political fray and — here's the rub — *who would never be directly responsible to the people.*

This meant that from henceforth the Canadian people were once again to have the spirit of their most important laws and moral traditions decided by people whom they did not place in power, and whom they would never be able to remove. In one stroke, Canadians were returned to the political condition that they had suffered prior to 1867. Morally and legally speaking, Canadians have become colonized again, and this time, not by a foreign power, but by their own hand.

This was a radical and deeply wrenching reorientation of Canada's entire judicial and political tradition, muscled into position by one man who was drawing from a tradition inimical to the English way of life. He was not citing Magna Carta, or Locke, or Blackstone, or Burke as his intellectual teachers. No. He repudiated the glories of the English tradition, and embraced instead the writings of Jean-Jacques Rousseau, the teacher of Marat, Robespierre, and Danton — radical intellectuals, socialists, and murderers all — hinting blithely as he did of Rousseau's concept of "the General Will," or in French *la volonté générale.*

In one of Trudeau's last publications, *Pierre Trudeau Speaks Out on Meech Lake,* he used that phrase repeatedly (and largely inaccurately, for I don't believe he ever really understood it). For example, on page 45 he urges Canada "to create a national will … *une volonté générale,* as Rousseau had called it." He did not realize that a national will is something subtly different from Rousseau's idea of a General Will. The former may be properly thrashed out in the heat of debate and passed by a majority, with disagreements tolerated. But the latter is a totalizing concept declared by edict of the supreme ruler (and Rousseau advocated the death penalty for all who opposed it once it was decided).

Nevertheless, this was but one of Trudeau's many references to Rousseau as his personal intellectual and moral authority. I do not hesitate to say that Rousseau's whole notion of the General Will was, and remains, a Franco-European conception of unitary national governance that is alien to the British way of life and to our entire inherited political history, if not (as many would argue) a precursor to much more sinister conceptions of governance, such as ones that nearly ended European civilization in the twentieth century.

In this way, Canada has been changed, uprooted, altered beyond recognition from its noble historical roots.

That is the real significance of the Charter.

THE RUSE OF POLITICAL APOLOGIES

The idea that all cultures are sleepwalking, and that history brings them to their senses after the fact, raises the distinct possibility that people in the present sit in judgment on their past selves as a form of self-absolution.

Is there a vague public awareness that we may be engaged in some unspecified evil at the moment, for which we could be taken to task by future generations? And if so, are we trying to alleviate the coming judgment by our children, so to speak, by apologizing now for the actions of those who came before us?

Why else are we judging our predecessors so harshly, and in such boldly self-confident moral terms? Why are present-day politicians so eager to pay off survivors (or their descendants) for actions or events deemed quite normal at the time, but considered sins today, with money that is not theirs? I am thinking of natives who attended residential schools a hundred years ago (almost all, voluntarily), or the Chinese head tax, or the Japanese internment during World War II.

It all seems a little bizarre, and a reversal of normal morality, which is like a universal law saying that those who do harm must pay. Instead, we, who did no harm, must apologize publicly for something over which we had no control, and politicians — who stand to gain by appearing morally upright — are extracting money from millions of citizens who were not even alive at the time, using it to pay off descendants who have suffered no harm, and whose only connection to the deemed sins of the past is their blood.

Let us be honest. It is far too easy — it is in fact exceedingly false and prideful — to judge the actions of our ancestors when we were not there living through their particular experiences. Indeed, something I find intriguing is the thought that in the very same circumstances, we would behave in much the same way.

For example, if we were part of a Christian missionary society in the north of Canada, we would probably think that residential schools were a good idea. Indeed, as mentioned, almost all residents of those schools wanted very badly to attend them. Instead, we are now a materialistic secular society, and our native population is confined to reserves where they have by far the highest murder, rape, drug, and alcohol abuse rates in Canada. This remains a dire scandal, and a waste of human potential on a scale the residential schools could never have approached.

As for the Chinese head tax? It all looks harsh from the vantage point of the present. But there is nothing to say a nation cannot charge a head tax on foreigners for any reason it wishes. Indeed, in recent times Canada has charged another head tax, in the form of a minimum requirement for personal assets of at least $100,000, to ... mostly Asian immigrants to Canada. This was not to build a railroad, but to build "the economy," a fiscal railroad.

And the Japanese internment? I think if the Japanese suddenly and brutally bombed Pearl Harbor in a cowardly sneak attack this weekend, thus declaring war on America — and especially if any Japanese shells landed on our own shores — as they did when a Japanese submarine shelled the Estevan Point lighthouse on Vancouver Island on June 20, 1942 — there would be panic. About thirty shells of 5.5 inch caliber were fired, and most missed the lighthouse. But the Japanese also launched nine thousand "fire balloons" into the Pacific Jet Stream that they intended to land on America and cause forest fires and urban chaos. About three hundred reached America. One child in Oregon died trying to fish one out of a tree, when it exploded. Some of these balloons also floated as far inland as Saskatchewan. My point is that it is very likely that in such a crisis we would do it all over again.

So I don't believe any of the apologies, because human nature being what it is, these actions, or worse, could happen again in the very same circumstances.

It is interesting to try to determine what human actions today our children will be apologizing for and paying for tomorrow. If I had to guess, I think they will be crying lots of tears for the native apartheid we are currently operating, at some eight billion dollars annually, which makes the residential school stuff look like a tea party.

And as my Jewish professor friend states so movingly, the Western democracies cannot be rescued from their incipient decline until their intellectuals come clean on their fellow-travelling with respect to the Soviet- and Chinese-communist holocausts. These, he rightly states, were ten or fifteen times as bad as the Nazi holocaust in terms of numbers liquidated, but Western intellectuals and so many sympathizers with socialism, past and present, have never been called to public account or apologized, nor ever admitted for a moment that they were dead wrong.

You see, there have always been, and will always be, lots of things for which a generation's children, and their children, will be able to apologize.

The Death of Cicero

In the absence of religious principle or commandment as a guide for behaviour, many people in our modern secular societies find themselves wondering what standard — other than their own personal wants — they might use to distinguish the good from the bad, and hence also to determine the legitimacy of the laws that govern them. This has been a concern of all civilizations. But it was a special concern of the ancient Romans, who felt that good law must be the very basis of society.

The Roman author and philosopher Cicero was a principal thinker in the development of something called "natural law," which he and many other thoughtful ancients considered a moral guideline in terms of which all human conduct and especially ordinary laws ought to be evaluated. Readers can experience this clash of legal concepts first-hand by reading Cicero's great speech *An Attack on an Enemy of Freedom*, now easily accessible in a small volume published by Penguin. Cicero paid a heavy price for speaking out: he was hunted down and assassinated by Mark Antony's soldiers.

The natural law has been suppressed during the last century and is often mocked in law schools today, and rarely taught. What replaced it was the concept of "positive law," which is basically the idea that a law is legitimate simply because a legitimate power says so.

But that concept ran into trouble at the post–World War II Nuremberg Trials, where so many German officers took refuge behind it, claiming that they were just following legitimate German law. The judges at Nuremberg were stymied, wondering on what basis they could condemn these war criminals. So they huddled. And when they returned, the defendants were stunned to hear that it didn't matter that they may have dutifully obeyed human law. The German courts, they were told, "recognized the necessity of universal higher standards," and any human law "loses all obligatory power if it violates the generally recognized principles of international law *or the natural law...*" (italics mine).

Or more simply put: if human law comes into conflict with true justice, "which is self-evident ... it must give way to justice." Why? Because, the judges said, natural justice automatically converts an unjust human law into "a lawless law."

Since then, natural law has been making a quiet comeback in the Western world. If we had to settle on a single sentence to define it, it could be this, adapted from Cicero himself: "*A command of right reason that follows nature for the common good.*" This standard recognizes that humans may often follow wrong reason, that a decision or law may turn against human nature, and that the common good may be overlooked in our judgments. But as a guideline, it is very strong.

What follows is the introduction to a chapter on natural law that I finished some months ago and which is part of a new work entitled *The Book of Absolutes*, to be published in the fall of 2008 by McGill-Queen's University Press. The peice attempts to capture the emotions and tensions surrounding the death of Cicero, in the hopes of interesting modern readers in the concept of natural law.

∾

This was the end. There had been weeks of flight and terror. And so a strange peace came over him when he glimpsed the first of many centurions through the window of his wind-swept villa at

Formiae. Bobbing heads and worn armour weaving between old rocks. They crept like scruffy animals, surrounding him. There would be no escape. His heart was filling with fear and love, his mind with triumphant sound. Everything he cherished gripped him at once. His children's sweet smiles. Graceful gulls carving the air hundreds of feet above a wild sea. His gardens, wild with dewy roses.

He felt suddenly faint, and it bothered him that his lips were sticking together. He had been warned so many times to remain silent; not to speak against Mark Antony, the mightiest of Rome. Even as he saw the door splintering and crashing inward and the glint of blades drawn, he felt the sharp indignity of such an end to a carefully crafted life. And a fleeting, remorseful irony, for silence had always been possible, and now he could not speak. But even if he could, he preferred to die rather than forsake the truth. And now, could he stand as bravely as he should, for the blade? Most certainly.

∽

After fleeing Rome for Greece, Marcus Tullius Cicero was driven back to shore by violent weather, and sought final refuge at his beloved villa on the west coast of Italy, where he was assassinated on December 7, 43 B.C., for the crime of speaking against tyranny. As Cicero lay in his own blood, the soldier Herrenius swiftly cut off his head and both hands for delivery to Mark Antony. When the tyrant's wife, Fulvia, saw Cicero's pallid face, she flew into a rage and pushed one of her long hairpins through his blue tongue. His head and hands were then nailed to the door of the Forum Rostra, where Rome's most famous orators had always spoken. It was a bloody lesson for any who dared follow his example.

Shortly afterward, with the masses silenced, Antony ordered the deaths of some three hundred Roman senators, and a couple of thousand of the most influential Roman citizens. Nothing could be clearer. Cicero stood for an unchanging higher natural law, a noble — and ennobling — legal and moral reality grounded in reason, nature, and the common good, a truth higher than any man, or any state; while Antony, like Caesar, stood for mere human law, which could be made, and remade, daily, if necessary, by whoever was in power. These opposing principles of law were at war then, and are still at war today.

THE NATURAL LAW IN A NUTSHELL

Research on natural law has always left me craving an answer to the simple question: What is it? It is hard to find a straightforward, brief explanation. So I tried writing one myself. Here it is. It is composed with the symbol > between the major arguments to suggest that they flow, one from the other, as linked and progressive conclusions, like stepping-stones.

∼

We exist in a universe that is governed by natural physical laws as are we. > But in addition to our physical being, we humans have a unique higher consciousness and reasoning capacity, enabling us to reflect on the meaning of existence and to discover the nature of the laws governing the material world and other forms of life, and that guide human action. > Consciousness and reason cannot be explained by materialism, because a merely material thing cannot pass judgment on or evaluate another material thing. > For this reason the human mind, which is the expression of consciousness, must be more than the material brain, and cannot be reduced to it. > Because all normal humans have a mind, they also have the capacity to reason rightly or wrongly, and hence the moral freedom to choose for good or for evil. > With this reason and moral freedom, humans everywhere and at all times have discovered a set of general natural laws or principles that they rely upon instinctively to guide individual and social existence. > This is only possible because in contrast to all lower animals, humans can comprehend cause and effect, the consequences of their actions, and many indubitable and universal truths of reason, such as the law of non-contradiction. > We see that all forms of being develop according to their natures, and move toward their own flourishing, or natural good, or happiness. This is the individual good of each individual being. > Humans differ from all other forms of being because although they have the capacity to discover the law of their own nature, they may then freely decide either to follow it or deny it. > Despite this capacity for denial, most humans everywhere strive for their own flourishing. > This is self-evidently best accomplished in human society where we exist as free and yet inescapably social beings. > As a social nature is common to all humans, we have a duty to care for our fellow beings and to promote — and resist threats to — the common good. > This combination of self-flourishing and the need for a common social existence results in the universal drive of all to preserve, protect, and extend life. > Accordingly, we have a natural desire for sexual unity, with the vast majority of us seeking procreation. > This framework of social life, reason, the common good, happiness, and procreation, leads to the discovery of the first and greatest of the natural laws: "Do good and avoid evil." > Arising from the foregoing are many other natural laws that preside as principles over our behaviour, such as honesty, refusing to steal, and respecting the basic moral worth of others, the centrality of the family, self-defence, treating others fairly, respecting property, the priority of the common good over individual will, and so on. These are expressed as commands or prohibitions in all societies of the world. > To this end, all societies universally respect certain moral and legal values such as courage, moderation, wisdom, justice, and might-does-not-make-right. > All of these values, and many more, indicate an intuitive grasp of the universal natural law as a standard of justice higher than human law. > This law is discovered as a common, universal outcome of free human beings participating in a search for the good. > All humans are able to understand through right reason (when acting for the common good according to nature, rather than against nature, or against the common good), the priority of this common good over their own personal wants. > This priority of the good, of justice and equity, etc., over personal wants, is why we can assert that such natural laws exist as transcendent principles, for we must have an idea of the good, of justice, of equity, in general before we ask what these are in particular situations. That is why we can say such laws are discovered, and not invented. > The consequence is that all humans must cultivate a higher self (guided by the compass of natural law) that seeks the common good and is based in right reason, to control or guide their wayward passions and unjust urges. > It follows from this that the state, which ought to be more than a collection of autonomous individuals — namely, a partnership for the common good — must do the same and be judged by the same standard, for the natural law itself is the higher self of the state. > Finally, as a consequence of their common human nature and social existence, we can see that all normal human beings carry the compass of natural law within: an innate sense concerning things like justice, fairness, equity, cheating, lying, love, courage, wisdom, and so on, that are understood universally as rough standards of moral conduct and right reason by which all human beings attempt to guide themselves.

This is the natural law.

V

Science

BIKING ON THE BRAIN

Recently, at 7 a.m. on a Sunday morning, a dozen cycling friends and I set off on a hundred-kilometer trip from Unionville, Ontario, to Lake Simcoe and back. Crispy cold beginnings in the morning mist, lots of excited chatter and bird-sounds, Canada geese overhead, and furtive glances to see who had new cycling equipment this year, talk of how out of shape we are this early in the season — normal guy stuff.

Leaving was easy, with a tailwind. Coming back — well, that was another story. Fortunately, my twenty-three year-old son Billy, who had spent many years telling me how he never wanted to cycle like his fanatical father but now is completely hooked, led most of the way back, on his seventeen-pound Cervelo. We averaged (and this detail is for cycling nuts) 19.2 miles per hour into a wind, which is pretty good for an aging group of enthusiasts.

At any rate, I mention this because you meet interesting people in endurance sports, where at certain points pain and extreme effort enter the equation and serve to readjust your temperament by way of induced humility. They are a more introspective lot. On Sunday, I rode for a time beside an fascinating fellow named Tom, who has a background in neuroscience and biology. Well, like me, Tom was writing a book, so we got into it right away, and before we knew it, twenty miles had gone by unnoticed. In my case the book was *The Book of Absolutes*, which included a chapter in which I attempt to set out the universals of biology.

It was clear in a flash that Tom and I came at this from opposing perspectives. "I don't believe there are any absolutes or universals in anything," he cheerfully announced.

Well, he certainly threw the cat amongst the pigeons with me, for I had spent about three years now trying to describe these very things as they manifest themselves in many aspects of life. Biology was a difficult subject area, because so many in the life sciences are evolutionists who take it as a matter of scientific religion, so to speak, that all forms of life evolve, and that therefore there can be no constants or universals.

"What about lipid membranes?" I asked. "What about the common genetic code of all species?"

And on it went. Where it got to be fun was in discussing the "brain" and the "mind." Tom, like me, and so many others, was raised a hard-core materialist. Over time, I became a disbeliever in this belief. But Tom is still convinced beyond a shadow of a doubt that all reality can be explained physically, and that nothing we call mystical or spiritual is real. For him (I hope I am rendering his beliefs accurately), we have a brain, and everything we are and do can be explained by drilling down into the deepest levels of neuroscience, where some physical explanation can always be found — if not today, then tomorrow. Although raised to believe this myself, I have had trouble with this purely physical view. But I also have trouble with the opposite — with the non-physical view of causation that some hold to the degree that they believe they can "heal" diseases by waving their hands a certain way, or concentrating their minds sincerely on the illness of someone who lives a thousand miles away.

Most of all, I think the mind and the brain are very different things. The "brain" is clearly material. If you open up a human head, it is full of matter. There is no little theatre in there where dreams happen, or where remembered events unfold, as they seem to, on a stage. The conclusion must be that the "mind," which needs a brain to operate at all, is something non-material. Just ask yourself, when you have a thought or a feeling, where is it located? Really — where do you think it is taking place? In the brain? Then where in the brain?

Most thoughts and concepts are spatial in nature, or "extended," as Descartes said. But the brain has no space in which to extend anything. And anyway, in terms of ordinary life, how is it possible for a thing such as a brain, or more specifically, a neuron, to act upon another thing? For example, put your hand on the table and lift any finger you choose. Or lift them all in some sequence, faster and faster, like a piano player. Now ask yourself, if the brain is all matter, and a finger is all matter (muscle, bone, nerves, etc.), then how can one thing order another thing to do anything? The standard school answer (which really avoids the deepest issue here) is that "the brain sends a signal along a nerve to the finger."

But, as I say, a pure thing cannot command another pure thing, and to be consistent, the pure materialist must argue that both entities, brain and finger, are just things. But then he is surely stuck for an answer. For if an entity "sends" a signal, a decision must be made, such as: send, or do not send.

And then there is the mental challenge of "the zombie world." In his latest book, *The Conscious Mind*, David Chalmers argues that from the purely materialist view, it is possible to imagine a zombie world that is only physical and can operate exactly as it does now, without any qualitative or subjective experiences present. But no one denies that subjective experiences do in fact exist, for we all have them. However, if we agree that the universe can operate just as it does without them, then subjective experiences must be something additional and non-physical. Something to ponder.

PHYSICS AND MYSTICS

I have just returned from a few days in beautiful Vancouver, where I got lucky because after almost five months of really terrible weather, it turned sunny and gorgeous. The city rose like a magical Atlantis above the sombre green of a devastated Stanley Park. There, some six thousand of the old stately trees that once towered over seemingly timeless trails had been felled by ferocious winter winds and lay twisted and belly up, so to speak. Another hundred years and maybe it will be as it once was.

In Vancouver, it is easy to feel overwhelmed by the grandness of visible nature. On this trip, I happened to be reading *Six Easy Pieces*, a book about quantum physics by the late Richard Feynman, and so I also felt overwhelmed by the *invisible* mysteries of nature.

Feynman won a shared Nobel Prize for physics in 1965 and taught at the California Institute of Technology until 1987. He was a quixotic, exuberant, and beloved teacher whose life was itself a manifestation of true philosophy: wonder incarnate. He mostly taught physics to advanced graduate students, but for the academic year 1962–1963, Cal Tech asked him to explain modern physics to undergraduates. And so in place of the usual stuff about levers, laws of motion, conservation of energy, and so on, he introduced students to the weird world of quantum physics, which is all about the behaviour of atoms, the many smaller particles within atoms, and how almost nothing in this *micro* world behaves as things do in the everyday *macro* world that we all know in the form of water, rocks, trees, chairs, tables, and so on. The book is a collection of the six easiest lectures, and for the uninitiated, they are a delight.

In a famous 1903 debate — which some say he lost — G.K. Chesterton argued for spirituality and the existence of God against the scientist Robert Blatchford, who argued for deterministic materialism and atheism. It so happened that long after the debate, Heisenberg published his "Uncertainty Principle," the gist of which was that we cannot predict the behaviour of subatomic particles, because if we know their position with certainty, we cannot know their momentum, and vice versa. Below I will try to suggest why this is true, for any readers who, like me, may have referred to this principle in the secret hope of impressing a listener, without really knowing what it was.

At any rate, when Blatchford read about the unpredictability of matter and energy (both apparently the same thing at this level, where "particles" are really bundles or "quanta" of energy), he published a confession that, due to the discovery of the Uncertainty Principle, he had now become "a spiritist." By this he meant that because no one could or would ever be able to predict the most fundamental behaviour of matter, only God could know the outcome of reality.

Something else must be added. The quantum revolution in physics took off by the 1920s and is known today as the New Physics, the Old Physics being what most of us learned (and still learn) in high school, composed of physical laws and equations that continue to govern the macro world we live in. Despite this fact — I mean that most of us will never see or hear about a quantum particle in our entire lives, and that Newton's laws will always govern everything we do — the much misunderstood themes of "relativity" and "uncertainty" in the New Physics almost immediately began to reshape public opinion about nature. Soon, sophisticated opinion insisted that "reality" is unknowable (and leapt to the conclusion that therefore truth is unknowable), even though quantum reality is not one that anyone could ever know or live in. What follows is the best explanation I can give for why there is an Uncertainty Principle in the micro world.

Werner Heisenberg first presented his principle in a letter to physicist Wolfgang Pauli in 1927, stating that in subatomic physics, it is impossible to know the exact position and the exact momentum of an object at the same time. The reason for this is that to know something about any particle, smaller particles must first be bounced off it, which then bounce back to the measuring device. This hitting and bouncing are so slight at macro levels that we say they are insignificant. Practically speaking, we could bounce all sorts of different things off objects to discover what they are like as long as we had a device to record the patterns made by the rebounding objects.

To observe a subatomic particle, however, we use light, which is itself made of packets of energy, or particles, called "photons." At the real-world or macroscopic level, when light bounces off an object, the reflection tells us exactly where the object is in space and time. But at a subatomic level, the photons that hit the particle cause it to move significantly — just like a billiard ball hitting another billiard ball — so that although its position may be measured accurately, its velocity will have been altered in performing this measurement of position. Accordingly, precise information about its true velocity is lost at the same moment. To know position more accurately is to know momentum less accurately, and vice versa.

This truth operates only at the subatomic level, and is of no concern or significance for the real world of macro-objects, which we can measure pretty accurately, and which have always and will always obey Newton's laws. This means that the fashionable modern penchant for describing the real world as one of uncertainty (and relativism) is a distortion of the human truth that the macro reality we experience never behaves this way. Its behaviour is certain to an amazing degree of Newtonian absoluteness, and it is simply wrong to imagine otherwise.

GLOBAL WARMING IN A NUTSHELL

The debate over so-called global warming is frustrating.

I am far from an expert, although I do read a fair amount of the science on this topic, and have kept a sizeable file on the pros and cons of the contentions about global warming over the years. My main concerns are the following. I think a good deal of the science is not up to a high standard, not because no earnest efforts are made, but because the subject matter (the entire Earth and surrounding atmosphere) is far too vast, the number of fluctuating variables and the time spans too great, and the whole business too shot through with political sensitivities (primarily of the anti-human, anti-population, anti-industry sort) that serious hypotheses can neither be framed nor tested in a controlled way.

On a political note, it is hard to escape the feeling that a great many global warming proponents are reflex leftists in their political beliefs, and anywhere from mildly to wildly anti-capitalist or even entirely opposed to all facets of Western civilization. Spiritually speaking, they usually fall in the camp of neo-romantic nature-lovers who, like most of us, despair at seeing their sweet Planet Earth fouled with human garbage, toxins, effluent, poisons, and the like. So they fight back by clinging to the dream of restoring the Garden of Eden, a beauteous Earth as it must have been before humans arrived.

There is no harm in this if a cleaner Earth can be gotten without harming civilization. The most radical of them, however, are intemperate and should be avoided, for they are green through and through, and consider human beings and their materialistic activities to be a kind of biological scourge or plague upon nature that must be eliminated. You can read some startling examples of this sort of talk at the end of this piece.

For less rabid sorts, however, the religion of nature is simply rooted in the ancient vision of the innocent and half-naked noble savage, free of all need and care, eating fresh fruit and sleeping under an oak tree, just after sipping his fill from a fresh babbling brook (or today, perhaps, from a bottle of Pinot Noir around the campfire). In short, at the back of this environmental consciousness (where dire warnings about global warming, excess human population, and filthy industrial activity are linked), a pristine purity beckons. I have felt its pull myself. Who hasn't? But it is precisely the presence — and prevalence — of certain of these unbalanced and pseudo-mystical motivations that turn up in the "science" of climate change, which suggests we ought to question all statements made about global warming (and many other environmentalist claims, too).

In what follows, there is an underlying question, namely, that given that all weather systems are chaotic by definition, and that humans have failed miserably at modelling and predicting the outcomes of even very limited chaotic systems such as river currents, wave action, or even fluctuating water pressure flowing through an ordinary pipe, or clouds forming overhead in the next few minutes, how is any prediction about such a vast and complicated subject possible?

IS THE EARTH WARMING OR COOLING?

The consensus now seems to be that some cooling, as well as warming, has occurred in the last century, and on balance, slightly more of the latter than the former. But I don't think anyone knows for sure, because on a daily basis the "temperature"

179

of Earth (here, you must specify land surface, ocean, mountain, or atmospheric temperatures) never stays the same.

On the sunny side of the globe, the sun's heat at some hundreds of degrees Celsius is intense and is, fortunately for us, prevented by our thin atmosphere from boiling our blood.

On the night side, the same atmosphere (thanks to its greenhouse effect) traps the heat raised in the day and, combined with the warmed-up soil, water, rock, and foliage, prevents cooling that otherwise at minus hundreds of degrees Celsius would freeze us solid by morning.

So the entire planet is rolling from exposure to extreme heat to cold every twenty-four hours. The result is that it is either warming or cooling in millions of different places all the time, night and day.

And so, despite what we hear from political agencies, such as the "Intergovernmental Panel on Climate Change" (IPCC) about conclusive proof of "global warming," not all climatologists agree. Some of those who disagree most energetically, such as Dr. Richard Lindzen, and those who participated in the BBC's "Great Global Warming Swindle" show of March 2007, were themselves contributors to the latest IPCC report. They say that the science in that report is unreliable at best, "because there is considerable uncertainty in current understanding of how the climate system varies naturally." As a result, they conclude, "Current estimates of the magnitude of future warming should be regarded as tentative and subject to future adjustments (either upward or downward)" (*National Post*, December 22, 2006).

So What Is the Future of the Planet?

With this question, it is wisest to take the long view. Throughout its geological history of some 4.5 billion years, the Earth has gone through at least twenty-five very long ice-age cycles, each involving about 90% cold weather, and about 10% warm weather. The six major periods of refrigeration have each lasted about fifty million years. Over the past eight hundred and fifty thousand years, ice ages have dominated the Earth's climate, interrupted by a few warm periods that have rarely exceeded twelve thousand years. It is now about eleven thousand years since the last ice age ended abruptly, and in a mere fifty to one hundred years, produced a climate much like what we have today. Talk about climate change!

With so much fear-mongering (which may be a species-protective instinct), it is easy to forget that in the early 1970s, in reaction to a short period of cooling from about 1940 to 1970, there developed a widespread "global cooling" hysteria, and a new ice age was widely predicted. Here are some quotes from that time:

> The cooling has already killed hundreds of thousands of people in poor nations.... If it continues it will cause world famine, world chaos, and probably world war, and this could all come by the year 2000. (U.S. Senator Claiborne Pell, cited in Lowell Ponte, *The Cooling*, 1976)

> ... The threat of a new ice age must now stand alongside nuclear war as a likely source of wholesale death and misery for mankind. (Nigel Calder, *International Wildlife*, 1975)

> Once the freeze starts, it will be too late. (Douglas Colligan, "Brace Yourself for Another Ice Age," in *Science Digest*, February 1973)

> According to the National Academy of Science's report on climate, we may be approaching

the end of a major interglacial cycle, with the
approach of a full-blown 10,000-year ice age a
real possibility. (*Science*, March 1, 1975)

I believe that increased rapid air pollution,
through its effect on the reflectivity of the
earth [sending heat back into space instead
of absorbing it] is currently dominant and is
responsible for the temperature decline of the
past decade or two. (Reid Bryson, "Environmental Roulette," in *Global Ecology*, 1971)

WHAT ARE GREENHOUSE GASES?

The label "greenhouse gases" was first used in the 1970s to
create the impression that man was fouling the atmosphere with
industrial gases that were "trapping" heat on Earth, which would
ordinarily escape into the upper atmosphere and dissipate into
space. But the fact is that most of the heat-trapping on Earth
(without which we would not have a habitable climate at all)
is done by natural water vapour found in the air, especially in
clouds, and also by carbon dioxide.

Without this natural atmospheric "greenhouse" (relatively
speaking, about the thickness of one layer of paint on a
basketball), we would sizzle to a cinder by day and freeze
solid by night. Oxygen and nitrogen, the two other major
atmospheric gases, do not trap heat. And although carbon
dioxide now has a bad name (I think a lot of people confuse it
with carbon monoxide, a deadly gas), it is actually a richly life-
enhancing substance (see below), without which there would
be no organic life possible on Earth. Indeed, all biological and
plant life on Earth is "carbon-based."

On this score, the current consensus is that the amount of
carbon dioxide in the atmosphere has indeed been increasing

over the past century, and the Earth's temperature has also risen about a half a degree Celsius in the past century (after accounting for ups and downs). However, a major point of conflict in the search for the cause of this rise has to do with confusion over cause and effect. Some, such as Al Gore (now of Nobel Laureate fame), infamously link the rise in temperature to the prior rise in CO_2 that he claims is due to increased industrialization and the burning of fossil fuels (said to be man-made, or "anthropogenic," causes).

But others argue that it is just the reverse. Natural temperature increases are due to normal causes such as solar radiation cycles, ocean current changes, and so on, and are followed by a natural rise in CO_2 levels, and not the other way around. The simple evidence for this is the fact that there have been many far warmer periods in the history of Earth, when there was rising temperature, followed by rising CO_2, but no industrialization whatever.

How Is Climate Change Measured?

There are many methods. But first, ask yourself: If you were given unlimited funding and reliable instruments, how would you measure the climate of "the globe"? Where should your measurements be taken, and at what time of day? Weather systems and temperatures are always local, so how would you average or blend all the readings to get a reliable number? After all, the oceans of the Earth are huge heat and cold reservoirs, and are millions of square miles in size, as are the vast deserts and icefields of Earth. Antarctica alone is 12.5 million square miles in extent. So where do you place your thermometers? On which mountain? In which valleys? Where on, or in, the oceans? Clearly, the vastest areas will be the least studied for the obvious practical reasons of inaccessibility.

As it happened, earnest climatologists placed lots of thermometers at airports and outside urban areas many decades ago, and have been peeking at them ever since. By now, about seventy million readings have been accumulated. Unfortunately for their "science," however, most of these instruments have been overtaken by urban sprawl and now sit in so-called heat islands caused by encroaching buildings, roads, plazas, and parking lots. So temperatures from these, the most numerous such stations on Earth, had to be "adjusted" to compensate for urbanization. Satellite measurements are apparently quite accurate, but they have shown either no change at all in the past fifty years since they came into use, or in many cases the degradation of these delicate instruments from cosmic radiation (or the decay of the orbits of the satellites themselves) has again called for "adjustments" to readings.

An even more damaging, if very human, problem with readings from surface temperature stations is that data are often taken only monthly, the time of day of such readings is often not known, and data from stations where readings are interrupted (Someone got sick? Ran out of snowmobile gas? Too many blackflies to go into the bush today?) are often thrown out of the mix, thus biasing the data. One study of an entire century of readings reported that after adjustments for such omissions and gaps, only 18.4% of the Earth's surface was covered by what was published as a "global" sampling (Michaels et al., 1998).

More damaging to current global warming theory, which predicts the warming of Earth's surface and therefore also a warming of the upper atmosphere, is that satellite readings by NASA (accurate to three one-hundredths of a degree Celsius!) show that atmospheric temperatures are cooling over the past twenty years, not warming. So why, contrary to theory, are surface temperatures rising a little, but atmospheric temperatures falling? No one knows. When other methods of tracking temperature changes are tallied from glacier ice-coring, tree-ring growth, coral layers, and so on (though all have been disputed in terms of accuracy), the weak consensus is that there was a twentieth-century warming from 1900 to about 1940 (of almost half a degree Celsius — long before most human greenhouse gasses were created), then there was a cooling from 1940 to about 1970, and then there was perhaps a warming trend again to the present. The upshot is that even if we can agree that "on average" there has been a half a degree of warming in the past century, most of it occurred prior to the recent rise in CO_2 levels.

But seriously, of what significance is this, for the long history of the Earth has shown a great number of "non-greenhouse" warmings and alternative coolings. For example, ice-coring and CO_2 measurements from the same sources show that some 135,000 years ago, there was a cooling of about eight degrees Celsius spread over a twenty-thousand year period, while CO_2 levels, which were at four times today's levels, did not lower at all (Rind, D., *Nature*, 363, 1992).

More embarrassing for current greenhouse theory is that during the Ordovician Age, four hundred and forty million years ago, CO_2 levels were ten times higher than they are today, and according to people like Al Gore, this should have produced a lot of warming. However, that period was an ice age, and vast ice sheets covered much of the Earth (up to 30% of Earth's surface, compared with today's 10%).

ARE CLIMATE MODELS ACCURATE?

Climate predictions are developed via a powerful computer program called a General Circulation Model (GCM). To put things in perspective, it is useful to recall that most probability models can handle two variables (such as cloud change and wind change) accurately. But when a third is introduced (such as water vapour change), the math gets very tricky and the predictions sloppier. Add a fourth, such as solar radiation, absorption, or reflectivity from an ever-changing cloud cover, and within those clouds, the changing volumes of vapour and particulate matter, and, and ... well, when we learn that today's climate models are tracking about five million variables, the heart sinks at the astonishing probabilities of large-scale error.

This is not surprising, given that most weather predictions today, even with the advantages of satellite views and infrared and radar imaging, often get the weather wrong for the coming weekend! Throw a few volcanic eruptions, such as Mt. Pinatubo (erupted in 1991) or Mt. St. Helens (May, 1980), into the mix, which can spew more greenhouse gasses into the atmosphere in twenty-four hours than have been put there in one hundred years of industrialization, and you get a good sense of the predictive unreliability at hand.

Mt. Erebus, which is on Ross Island in Antarctica, was estimated to have spewed over 1,000 tonnes of chlorine per day between 1976 and 1983, which is almost two-thirds of the entire world production of chlorofluorocarbons (the major villain in erosion of the ozone layer). This estimate has been greatly reduced since, but such variations give a sense of what Mother Nature can do. Further to this, all climate models rely on climate "parameters" programmed into the computer model and accurate assessment of "feedback mechanisms" (what does the model say will happen if we double CO_2?). Not much is known about real-world feedback, so whatever is used in such models comes from estimating.

This produces a field day for computer geeks and catastrophists because you can model anything you want to see and then go around saying that this is what will happen because the model says so. In their attempts to face this problem (in which the computer model is a kind of psychogram of the scientist's imagination), serious climatologists who just want to guesstimate something close to the possible future outcomes include adjustments for things like "heat flux." But such "artificial flux tuning" can themselves introduce large biases in data, as can and do biases in calculation of water vapour levels, cloud cover, storm activity, ocean to surface interactions, and feedback from snow and ice cover. So a simple summary of this situation would be to say that there are a lot of fanciful computer models out there chasing elusive and fluctuating data.

WHAT IS THE EFFECT OF SOLAR AND COSMIC RADIATION?

Scientists looking for the principal cause of rises in temperature that cannot be due to human activity (such as occurred between 1910 and 1940) point to the increased brightness of the sun. Obviously, all of Earth's energy systems are solar-driven, and so variations in solar radiation have a profound effect on our climate. The surface magnetism of the sun is measurable and shows a clear eleven-year cycle, during which brightness rises and dims according to the rise and fall of solar-surface magnetism (from NASA satellite data). Records of the rise and fall of Earth's surface temperatures over the past two hundred and forty years track these changes in solar radiation very closely — though no one knows whether the influence of solar radiation is short (decades) or long-term (centuries).

Also, for unknown reasons, every two centuries or so (confirmed by radiocarbon tests and other means) the sun's magnetism level and brightness drop significantly for a few decades (this is called a "Maunder Minimum"), as it did from 1640 to about 1720, during which period Earth's temperature went down one degree Celsius. This "Little Ice Age" ended about 1860.

Renowned climatologist Professor Tim Patterson of Carleton University in Ottawa warns that the next weak solar cycle will be hitting us about 2020, and we ought to be concerned because "no one is farming north of us" (*Calgary Sun* (!),

May 18, 2007). He also states that things warmed up considerably after the Little Ice Age until about 1940, "with no help from carbon dioxide." After that, cooling took place until about 1970, even though CO_2 "was going up like crazy." Patterson says, "There is no correlation between warming and CO_2." He suspects that any warming not explained by solar radiation is due to patterns of cosmic radiation, which constantly bombard Earth. Cosmic particles tend to create more cloud cover and so more cooling. But when the sun is in a bright cycle as at present, solar radiation blows away the cosmic particles and we get warming (for now).

One theory now given a good deal of credence is that Earth's climate results from the combined effect of the changing shape of Earth's orbit around the sun from circular to elliptical over a period of one hundred thousand years (resulting in a variation of distance from or proximity to the sun of some twenty-thousand kilometers); the wobble of the Earth's axis itself (the pole wanders in a circle over a twenty-six-thousand-year period); and the difference in the Earth's equatorial and orbital planes, which varies a few degrees every forty thousand years; and ... these things combined correlate highly with the Earth's ice ages.

On a final note, an observation that seems to support the solar and cosmic radiation emphasis is that Mars, the only other planet to show its climate secrets, has been experiencing a warming along with us, and its polar ice sheets have been visibly diminishing. Dr. Abdussamatov, a senior member of the Russian Academy of Sciences, says, "Mars has global warming but without a greenhouse and without the participation of Martians" (*National Post*, January 6, 2007). The warming here and there, he insists, "can only be a straight-line consequence of ... a long-time change in solar irradiance," which explains the increased volume of CO_2 emissions (due to a warming of the oceans and thus a release of stored CO_2).

He explains that the common view that man's industrial activity is the deciding factor in global warming "has emerged from a misinterpretation of cause and effect relations," and notes that heated man-made greenhouse gasses, which become lighter due to expansion, rise in the atmosphere, and give their absorbed heat away.

But the real news, he warns, is that the heating of Earth's oceans due to solar irradiation, which has now begun to fall, has reached its peak and is now also falling. This solar cycle will reach its weakest irradiance around 2040, after which there will be an inevitable deep freeze on Earth, lasting for about fifty years. Then temperatures will rise again.

What Will Happen If Ice at the Poles Melts?

Most of the ice on Earth is at the two poles. At the North Pole, almost all the ice is floating in water. And from Archimedes' principle, we know that anything floating in water displaces its own weight in water. So an ice cube dropped into a glass of water will cause a little rise in the level of water in the glass because the cube has pushed the water up by displacement. But as the ice cube melts, the higher level will remain exactly the same. It will not go up or down, because whether you add two ounces of liquid water to a glass, or two ounces of frozen water, the amount is the same. If all the ice at the North Pole that is floating in water — most of it — melts tomorrow, the sea levels of the Earth will not be changed in any way. Not one inch. Not a millionth of an inch.

That can only happen if ice that is resting on land up there melts and flows as new water into the oceans. So much for the North Pole. The average annual temperature in the high Arctic is minus thirty-four degrees C. On top of this, a forty-year record of Arctic temperature by Americans and Russians from 1950 to 1990 showed a cooling trend of 1.5 degrees C (Kahl,

Nature, 361, 1993). In short, it is a little hard to fathom why a global rise of one degree down here in the next century would change much up there.

As for the South Pole, the massive amounts of ice there — most of the world's store of ice — is indeed resting on land. But the average altitude of Antarctica is about seven thousand feet, in places exceeding fifteen thousand feet, and the average annual temperature is somewhere around minus fifty degrees C. The ice has been sitting there for several hundred million years, is so large it forms its own microclimate, gets sunlight at a narrow angle for only six months a year, and like other major ice sheets is remarkably resistant to melting. There is no known mechanism that could melt such a mass of ice. A warming of Earth, even if it occurs at levels of a few degrees Celsius, will not change much on a continent that is averaging minus fifty degrees C.

As for the alarmist photos of "shelf" ice melting in Antarctica? It is already floating in water and so, as at the North Pole, the same amount of displacement occurs whether it sits in the water as ice today, or as melted ice, or water, tomorrow. To top it off, studies have shown that Antarctica has actually been cooling recently. For the two decades prior to 2000, satellites recorded a cooling of 0.42 degrees C and land units recorded 0.008 degrees C (Comiso, 2000, and Watkins and Simmonds, 2000).

What Is the Connection Between Carbon Dioxide and Temperature Change?

It is disputed. In Al Gore's very slick film *An Inconvenient Truth*, the central case presented is that the clear rise in atmospheric CO_2 is the cause of a parallel rise in the Earth's surface temperature (but this is not so in the upper atmosphere, as mentioned above — on which fact Gore is slickly silent). However, it bears repeating that many climatologists of high repute insist that the relationship is the reverse. To complicate matters, there has been a general warming trend for the past three hundred years since the Little Ice Age, and CO_2 levels have tended to track this.

What greatly frustrates the prophets of doom in our midst, however, is the truth of the so-called Medieval Warming Period — a centuries-long period over one thousand years ago, when the Earth was much warmer than today — about two degrees C — in the complete absence of any man-made greenhouse gasses, except from gaseous cows, horses, and humans. That was when the Vikings settled Greenland, then withdrew when another cooling arrived.

Even more embarrassing is the fact that scientists such as John Matthews from Canada's Geologic Survey reported finding fossils of pine trees and even tropical vegetation and biological organisms in the High Arctic, around Ellesmere Island, some four hundred miles from the North Pole. And the same year, Ohio University's Peter Webb dug up three-million-year-old roots and leaves of beech trees from a mountain four hundred miles from the South Pole (*Toronto Star*, June 16, 1991). And fossils of dinosaurs found in the High Arctic are plentiful and on display in many museums. The Arctic sea temperature fifty-five million years ago was around eighteen degrees Celsius, and later, during what is called the "super-greenhouse" period, sea temperatures there rose to twenty-three degrees C (*National Post*, June 1, 2006). For a reality warp, try to imagine Eskimos in bikinis!

How Much CO_2 Are We Talking About?

CO_2 (which amounts to about 0.07% of the entire atmosphere) is tallied in gigatons of carbon (GtC). A gigaton is a billion metric tons, or a trillion kilograms. The recent annual increase in global carbon attributed to human activities has been estimated at roughly 6.52 GtC. But to understand what this means, we have to ask how much natural carbon there is to begin with, and where it is, and how fast it moves from place to place. Estimates are that the Earth's atmosphere contains around 750 GtC; the surface of oceans contains about 1000 GtC; the intermediate and deep oceans about 38,000GtC; and the Earth's natural vegetation cover and other stuff lying around contains about 2,200 GtC. Carbon moves naturally from one place to another: about 90 GtC per year move between oceans and air; about 60 GtC between vegetation and air; about 50 GtC between marine life and ocean surfaces; and between surface and deep ocean levels about 100 GtC.

So great is the magnitude of these reservoirs of carbon, and the rate of production and absorption between them, that no accurate number can be placed on the amount of man-made carbon present on Earth. Nor can a source of the recent rise in atmospheric carbon be determined. Reliable research tells us that in historical terms, concentrations of CO_2 have varied widely over geological time, with peaks as much as twenty times higher than at present, and troughs at eighteenth-century levels. And incidentally, each human being exhales about one hundred thousand litres of CO_2 per year, which comes to about a third of the amount expelled by the five hundred million automobiles on Earth, and to that we have to add the 150 gigatons of CO_2 from the breathing of the billions of animals on Earth.

How Do Plants Respond to CO_2 Enrichment?

Very favourably. Controlled experiments with environments, in which plants such as orange trees and wheat are grown in, um, greenhouses, and force-fed carbon at very high levels of enrichment, produce astonishing results — as much as tripling their rate of growth. In one experiment, sour orange trees had a growth rate 170% faster than normal, and orange production was 127% greater. All plants seem to respond energetically to carbon fertilization, especially trees, because carbon is a nutrient, or food, for all organic life on Earth, and not a pollutant or some evil gas as we tend to believe, due to its recent bad press. Indeed, some reading on this topic produces the feeling that the Earth is presently relatively carbon-poor, and that more of it would help feed millions of hungry human beings.

Some Quotes on Climate Science from the Top

Professor Willie Soon, Astrophysicist, from the Harvard-Smithsonian Center for Astrophysics, and co-author of a major Harvard study of 240 climate studies showing warming and cooling variability long before the industrial age, says that policy makers should use "strong caution in finding a human fingerprint" in climate change. (*National Post*, April 8, 2007)

Professor Emeritus Antonino Zichichi, Advanced Physics, University of Bologna, President of the World Federation of Scientists, complained of climate models in general, and of the IPCC report in particular, stating that the kind of models used in that report "are incoherent and invalid from a scientific point of view."

Patrick Moore, co-founder of Greenpeace: "It's a political activist movement," and anyone who disagrees with the anti-capitalist global-warming theory is considered "like a holocaust denier."

Professor Reid Bryson, Fellow of the American Association for the Advancement of Science on

Global Warming: Man-made global warming "is a theory for which there is no credible proof." And on Al Gore's movie *An Inconvenient Truth*: "Don't make me throw up. It's not science. It's not true."

SOME RADICAL GREEN IDEAS

Here are some of the anti-humanist sentiments I found in my files, from when all this was getting started, around 1993.

Here is David Bower, anti-population spokesman for Friends of the Earth: "*Childbearing should be a punishable crime against society, unless the parent holds a government licence.*"

Carol Amery, of the German Green Party, says that she and her colleagues "*aspire to a cultural model in which the killing of a forest will be considered more contemptible and more criminal than the sale of six-year-old children to Asian brothels.*" Huh? I mean, that is a strange mind indeed: Can't she empathize with those children?

Stephanie Mills, a co-author of the book *Whatever Happened to Ecology?*, insists that "*humanity is debased protoplasm.*"

Paul Watson of the Sea Shepherd operation told the press that "*humanity is the AIDS of the earth.*"

And finally, from perhaps the most rabidly anti-human of them all, David Graber, a research biologist with the American National Parks Service, comes these words: *"Human happiness [is] not as important as a wild and healthy planet. We have become a plague upon ourselves and upon the earth. Until such time as homo sapiens should decide to rejoin nature, some of us can only hope for the right virus to come along."*

David seems to imagine he would survive the virus he is wishing on the rest of us.

Sources: In addition to the many articles and news sources collected in my files over the years, much of the data and insight in this piece was taken from publications such as The Fraser Institute's *Global Warming: A Guide to the Science* (2001), as well as the excellent scientific papers collected by the Institute in *Global Warming: The Science and the Politics* (1997), and also from various sources published by the Marshall Institute, USA.

Printed in the United States
138858LV00002B/12/A